LEEDS
LEGENDS

LEEDS LEGENDS

DAVID SAFFER

TEMPUS

ACKNOWLEDGEMENTS

Grateful thanks to the following people and organisations for their help with this publication: Leeds United Football Club, Mike Fisher and Jayne Marsden at Yorkshire Post Newspapers Ltd; James Howarth and Holly Bennion at Tempus Publishing Ltd. Statistician Gary Shepherd has produced all the career statistics for this book. His expertise and efforts are greatly appreciated.

Images for this publication have been supplied by Yorkshire Post Newspapers Ltd. Every effort has been made to identify the original source of other illustrations. For questions regarding copyright contact Tempus Publishing Ltd. This book is dedicated to my number one team: Deborah, Daniella, Abigail and Jake.

Frontispiece: Revie's dream team, August 1969. From left: Lorimer, Charlton, Clarke, Jones, Gray, Madeley, Cooper, Hunter, Giles, Reaney, Sprake, Bremner.

First published 2004

Tempus Publishing Ltd
The Mill, Brimscombe Port
Stroud, Gloucestershire GL5 2QG
www.tempus-publishing.com

© David Saffer, 2004

British Library Cataloguing in Publication Data.
A catalogue record for this book is available from the British Library.

ISBN 0 7524 2700 8

Typesetting and origination by Tempus Publishing.
Printed and bound in Great Britain

FOREWORD

BY JOHN CHARLES CBE

My association with Leeds United may go back over fifty years, but I can still remember how thrilled I was when manager Major Frank Buckley signed me on my sixteenth birthday. After making my debut at the end of the 1948/49 season, I went on to play eight years for Leeds. They were enjoyable days.

I recall the excitement among fans when we reached the FA Cup quarter-finals for the first time in the club's history, but my favourite memory was winning promotion to the First Division in 1956 when Raich Carter was in charge. It was a wonderful year for us because we had been out of the top division for a long time and it had been the club's main aim since I arrived at Elland Road.

Originally I played in defence, but Major Buckley, who came up with lots of 'fantastic' ideas, decided to put me at centre forward when someone was injured and brought Jack Charlton in at centre half. I enjoyed my time as a defender, but there was no better feeling than scoring a goal. I'm very proud of the goalscoring records I set at Leeds, especially the 42 league goals I scored in 1953/54; it certainly gives today's strikers something to aim at!

Although I notched many goals over the years for Leeds, one of my favourites, and I think my best, came against Doncaster Rovers at Elland Road during our promotion season. I remember getting the ball and going on a long run where I had to beat five or six players before scoring. Another match that I have never forgotten was the day I scored a hat-trick of headers. It was special because it is rarely achieved.

We had a number of good players in our side with the likes of Eric Kerfoot, Jack Charlton at centre half, Jimmy Dunn at full-back, Roy Wood in goal, David Cochrane at outside right, Albert Nightingale at inside left and Harold Williams on the wing. When we got promotion we did really well during our first season, finishing eighth. We did not think we would finish that high.

Juventus then paid a world record £65,000 fee for me and I had some terrific years there. I was voted Italy's 'Footballer of the Year' as Juventus won three championships and the Italian Cup. They were wonderful days.

To gain my first Welsh cap at eighteen was incredible, and among many highlights, I played in the 1958 World Cup finals in Sweden. There were some great players during my era, including the likes of Puskas, Pelé, and my personal favourite Di Stefano; who was the best I ever faced.

The welcome I received in Leeds and Turin throughout the years always amazed me because it happened such a long time ago. They were great times and I have many wonderful memories. I am pleased I helped Leeds gain some success and I loved my time in Italy. In the modern game, the ball is a bit lighter and so are the boots. I would love to see today's stars play in our kit!

When David asked me to write this foreword, I was delighted to oblige. Since the club's formation many great players and a number of managers have contributed to the Leeds United story. I know you will enjoy reading about their deeds on behalf of a great club.

John Charles

INTRODUCTION

The 'beautiful game' in Leeds began during the latter half of the nineteenth century when a succession of clubs attempted to establish football as a major sport in the city. Success would not come though until an historic meeting on 30 August 1904 at the Griffin Hotel, Boar Lane, when fifty people were told, 'the time is ripe for a good association club in Leeds'. With optimism high, a resolution to form Leeds City, based at Elland Road, was passed.

A member of the West Yorkshire League in 1904/05, Leeds City gained election to the Football League (formed in 1888) on 29 May 1905 and competed in the Second Division until they were expelled from the league by the Football Association in October 1919 after allegations of illegal payments to players. Leeds United surfaced from the ashes of the disgraced club. Voted into the Midland League on 31 October 1919, the newly formed club joined the Second Division of the Football League on 31 May 1920.

Throughout the past 100 years, players have represented Leeds City and Leeds United with distinction. However, *Leeds Legends* is not only about the likes of Billy McLeod, Fred Croot, Jim Baker, Ernie Hart, Willis Edwards, John Charles, Bobby Collins, Billy Bremner, Jack Charlton, Norman Hunter, Eddie Gray and Gordon Strachan. Managers such as Arthur Fairclough, Don Revie and Howard Wilkinson, and chairmen like Hilton Crowther and Harry Reynolds have also contributed in creating club folklore. Each biopic in *Leeds Legends* summarises an individual's attributes and achievements, and I have encapsulated the era in which they served.

Nominating players that have starred during this period has been an impossible task at times because there are so many candidates. I was not surprised though, because discussing this topic with supporters of different generations failed to produce a definitive list as everyone values loyalty, commitment, influence and skill differently.

I decided in the end to include virtually every footballer who has made 200 appearances for Leeds City or Leeds United. In addition, selecting players who made a major impact in a brief spell or demonstrated unswerving loyalty over a number of years completed my mission. Whether battling for honours domestically or in Europe, fighting relegation or displaying their skills during a transitional era, all thrilled supporters in their heyday.

At the inception of *Leeds Legends* in 2002, I was honoured when the greatest all-round footballer to grace Leeds United, John Charles, agreed to contribute the foreword. World class at centre half and centre forward, the Gentle Giant's goalscoring exploits fifty years ago during the 1953/54 campaign still stand. Although records are set to be broken, nobody has come close to matching his 42 league goals or five hat-tricks in a season. Recognised as one of football's all-time greats, his death earlier this year saddened everyone involved in the game, but his memory will live on forever.

The last century has seen supporters follow Leeds City and Leeds United through thick and thin, and as a new century dawns this scenario will continue. Researching material for this book has been enlightening. I hope you enjoy reading the finished product 100 years on from the formative days of professional football in the city of Leeds.

David Saffer, 30 August 2004

ROLE OF HONOUR

Jimmy Armfield
Neil Aspin
Ian Baird
Jim Baker
Mick Bates
David Batty
Rod Belfitt
Mick Bates
Lee Bowyer
Billy Bremner
Tommy Burden
Raich Carter
Eric Cantona
Lee Chapman
Herbert Chapman
John Charles
Jack Charlton
Trevor Cherry
Allan Clarke
David Cochrane
Tom Cochrane
Bobby Collins
Terry Cooper
Wilf Copping
Fred Croot
Hilton Crowther
Tony Currie
Mervyn Day
Tony Dorigo
Bert Duffield
Harry Duggan
Jimmy Dunn
Willis Edwards
Arthur Fairclough

Chris Fairclough
Brian Flynn
Billy Furness
Johnny Giles
Arthur Graham
Eddie Gray
Frank Gray
Jimmy Greenhoff
Grenville Hair
Ernie Hart
Ian Harte
Paul Harte
David Harvey
Jimmy Floyd
Hasselbaink
George Hodgson
Tom Holley
Norman Hunter
Arthur Hydes
Tom Jennings
Albert Johanneson
Mick Jones
Joe Jordan
Charlie Keetley
Gary Kelly
Eric Kerfoot
Harry Kewell
Peter Lorimer
John Lukic
Gary McAllister
Duncan McKenzie
Billy McLeod
Gordon McQueen
Paul Madeley

Nigel Martyn
Bill Menzies
George Milburn
Jack Milburn
Jim Milburn
Mike O'Grady
David O'Leary
Alan Peacock
Jimmy Potts
Lucas Radebe
Dick Ray
Paul Reaney
Don Revie
Harry Reynolds
Andy Ritchie
John Sheridan
Alan Smith
Gary Speed
Gary Sprake
Mel Sterland
Jim Storrie
Gordon Strachan
Bobby Turnbull
Mark Viduka
Russell Wainscoat
Rod Wallace
David Wetherall
Chris Whyte
Howard Wilkinson
Harold Williams
Roy Wood
Tony Yeboah
Terry Yorath

JIMMY ARMFIELD

Jimmy Armfield took the helm at Leeds United following Brian Clough's shambolic forty-four-day stay at Elland Road in October 1974. It was a huge task, having the responsibility of breaking-up Don Revie's legendary squad. However, calm and dignified, and possessing a first-rate footballing brain, 'Gentleman Jim' methodically created an attractive, competitive and organised side that went close to honours, which said much for his managerial ability.

Born in Blackpool, in September 1935, Armfield enjoyed a distinguished career for Blackpool, making 568 appearances. A stalwart defender for England, winning 43 caps, Armfield captained his country on numerous occasions and was a key player in the side that reached the quarter-finals of the 1962 World Cup finals before losing to eventual winners Brazil. He was also a member of the victorious 1966 World Cup-winning squad. Following his retirement as a player, Armfield steered Bolton Wanderers to the Third Division title in 1972/73 in his first post as a manager.

His success brought him to the attention of the Leeds United board, but at thirty-eight Armfield was unquestionably inexperienced in managerial terms when he inherited the monumental task of replacing the likes of Billy Bremner, Johnny Giles and Norman Hunter. Undeterred, Armfield took on the challenge systematically.

In his first season at the helm, Armfield altered little, apart from drafting in Clough's best signing Duncan McKenzie and giving Frank Gray his first extended run in the first team. The players responded. Quickly stabilising the 1974/75 league campaign after an appalling start, Leeds powered their way to the European Cup final, defeating Barcelona in a memorable semi-final clash. Following riots by a section of Leeds fans at the end of the defeat against

Leeds United 1975/76. Jimmy Armfield, manager, extreme left.

Bayern Munich, Armfield's input during an appeal to UEFA was significant in the club's European ban being cut to two years.

The mid-1970s saw the likes of Tony Currie, Arthur Graham, Ray Hankin and Brian Flynn come into the side and to their credit, considering the era they had to follow, Armfield's players produced exciting football. Of his side, the flamboyant Currie was undoubtedly his best signing, orchestrating a number of sensational displays. Ultimately though, the board grew impatient, dismissing him at the end of the 1977/78 season after his third full year in charge, even though domestically he had guided the team to the semi-finals of both the League Cup and FA Cup.

An opinion at the time suggested that Armfield was too relaxed, that he didn't have the cutting edge to take Leeds forward. There was also a standing jibe that the manager's indecision was final! That notion was harsh though, because breaking-up Revie's star-studded team required an open chequebook and then there were no guarantees. In very trying circumstances, with no future stars in the youth set-up, Jimmy Armfield did a great job for Leeds United.

One of the most respected personalities still involved in the game, Armfield is an advisor to the Football Association and one of football's most popular pundits when commentating on matches for BBC Radio Five Live around the world.

Neil Aspin is one of Leeds United's youngest debutants at just sixteen. Popular with supporters, Aspin was an honest, hard-working defender who gave everything during a game. He also had incredible endurance throughout a match.

Born in Gateshead on 12 April 1965, Aspin won Durham county school honours and had trials with England Schoolboys before joining Leeds as an apprentice. Allan Clarke gave him his first-team opportunity during the 1981/82 season when he drafted him into the first team at short notice to face Ipswich Town at Elland Road.

Following the club's relegation to the Second Division, the youngster had to wait two years before Eddie Gray gave him an extended run in the side. Once in the first team however, Aspin developed into a reliable defender, generally at centre half or right-back and became one of the side's most steady performers.

A resolute defender, he used his speed and strength to not only make last-ditch tackles, but also to join in with the attack from the right flank. Commanding in the air, a goal from Aspin was a rare treat for supporters; indeed he only managed six during his time at Leeds, the most important coming against Shrewsbury Town in November 1986, which won a hard-fought encounter.

Consistent throughout his years at Elland Road, Aspin's most memorable season was in 1986/87 when Billy Bremner was at the helm. In a thrilling campaign, Leeds battled their way to the semi-finals of the FA Cup and reached the Second Division play-off final. The team's run to the last four not only surprised soccer pundits, but also Aspin himself, who had to postpone his wedding plans to play against Coventry City! Agonisingly, Coventry won a classic match 3-2, and in the last game of the season Charlton Athletic scored two late goals in extra time to win a nail-biting encounter. It was a cruel end to an unforgettable campaign.

The arrival of Mel Sterland in July 1989 ultimately resulted in Aspin's departure to Port Vale for £200,000 during the close season after 240 (+4 substitute) appearances. He went on to serve the 'Valiants' with distinction for ten seasons, helping them claim the Autoglass Trophy at Wembley in 1993. Naturally fit, Aspin moved back to the North-East to serve both Darlington and Hartlepool prior to joining Harrogate Town as player-coach in 2000.

Player of the Year in 1984/85, Neil Aspin was a dedicated professional. Although not creating headlines like his colleagues, Aspin was a key member of Gray and Bremner's defence, and supporters appreciated his efforts during a difficult period in the club's history.

I an Baird, during two spells at Leeds United in the 1980s, was renowned for his direct approach in leading the line. A strong, burly centre forward, Baird always made life difficult for opponents, who found him a handful to mark.

Born in Rotherham, 1 April 1964, Baird played for England Schoolboys before joining Southampton as an apprentice in 1980. Although he signed professional terms two years later, he didn't make an impact and after loan spells at Cardiff City and Newcastle United was snapped up by Eddie Gray for £75,000 in March 1985.

Following his debut against Portsmouth, Baird impressed immediately with 6 goals in as many games, including a brace against Wimbledon as Leeds finished the season promisingly in seventh place. However, a poor start in 1985/86 saw Billy Bremner take up the reigns at Elland Road. The new boss believed that Baird's determination, aggression, aerial power and no-nonsense approach at centre forward would make him an asset to his team. Bremner was proved correct as Baird became a firm favourite with supporters, and in tandem with John Sheridan and Andy Ritchie an understanding quickly developed.

Baird heads home against QPR in an FA Cup clash.

Baird finished the campaign as top scorer, a feat he repeated in 1986/87 with 19 goals, including a hat-trick against Plymouth Argyle. The campaign was memorable for everyone connected with the club as Leeds battled their way to the FA Cup semi-finals and Second Division play-off final. Although both games were lost in extra time, it had been a pulsating season.

The exposure received resulted in clubs taking an interest in Baird, and with Leeds still in the Second Division he joined First Division-bound Portsmouth for £285,000. Financial problems at Fratton Park meant a quick return to Elland Road and Bremner wasted little time, paying £100,000 less than Portsmouth had paid Leeds.

Baird's second spell at Leeds began positively alongside Bobby Davison and John Pearson, and continued initially when Howard Wilkinson replaced Bremner. Voted Player of the Year in 1988/89, his brave match-winning header in the opening months of the 1989/90 season against Newcastle United was typical of the player.

Despite having a tendency to make impulsive tackles and get embroiled in heated exchanges, resulting in far too many bookings, fans appreciated his wholehearted displays. Baird played his part as Wilkinson's new-look side moved into pole position in the race for promotion, but he was not a goal machine and Wilkinson's ruthless drive for a cutting edge in attack signalled an end to his time at Leeds with the arrival of Lee Chapman.

Baird's transfer to Middlesbrough for £400,000 meant a new challenge, fighting relegation instead of battling for promotion. However, in an amazing twist his brace against Newcastle United on the last day of the season not only saved his new club from relegation, but also consigned their neighbours to the play-offs!

Of course, his goals weren't needed by Leeds but the news eased nerves for thousands of Leeds fans before Chapman made promotion and the title secure at Bournemouth. Although Baird ultimately missed the subsequent celebrations, his efforts during the season were rewarded with a Second Division championship medal. As Leeds powered their way to a new era, Ian Baird went on to play for a number of clubs, including Hearts, but it is his five years at Leeds when he scored 57 goals in 190 (+2 substitute) games that were his most rewarding as a footballer.

JIM BAKER

Leeds United 1923/24 Division Two Champions. Jim Baker is seated second from left.

Jim Baker was Leeds United's first captain and the man who led the team to their first honour in 1923/24; the Second Division championship. His consistency during the club's formative years was quite astonishing. In the first three seasons, Baker was the only member of the team to play in all 126 league fixtures and would uniquely take part in the first 149 Football League encounters!

Born in Staffordshire on 15 November 1891, Baker was one of three 'footballing' brothers. Aaron Baker had brief spells at Leeds, Sheffield Wednesaday and Luton Town while Alf Baker enjoyed success at Woolwich Arsenal and represented England. Meanwhile, Jim enjoyed spells at Portsmouth, Hartlepool and Huddersfield Town prior to joining Leeds in 1920 when ex-Town manager Arthur Fairclough brought him at Elland Road.

Nicknamed 'T'Owd War 'Oss', Baker was a resolute centre-back and a commanding presence in defence, and during Leeds United's early years his experience was vital to the club's development. He made his Leeds debut against Port Vale on the opening day of the 1920/21 campaign, the club's first ever Football League match, and during this historic season was one of three players, alongside Billy Down and Albert Duffield, to be ever present.

The campaign also brought his only goals for the club, both winning penalties in tight games that Leeds won, against Birmingham City 1-0 and Clapton Orient 2-1. A neat player, solid in the air and assured, Baker quickly developed a solid foundation alongside full-backs Duffield, Jimmy Frew, and Ernie Hart in the heart of defence.

By 1923/24 Leeds had a settled team and during an unforgettable campaign, top-flight football was achieved for the first time in the club's short history. Promotion seemed on the cards following two winning streaks; however, the title would only be claimed in the penultimate game of the season against Nelson. The title success was Baker's finest achievement as a Leeds player.

Life was not easy in the First Division as Fairclough's team struggled near the foot of the table. It was also clear that Baker's best days were behind him and, after 9 appearances in 1925/26, he left Leeds having played 208 games. Baker played briefly for Nelson and Colne Valley before retiring from the game but his connections with Leeds United were not over as he scouted for the club during the 1950s and served as a board member between 1959 and 1961.

One can only imagine the excitement there must have been when the club played its first ever game. The decision to make Jim Baker, who died in 1966, the club's first captain, is historically one of the most significant in the Yorkshire club's eighty-five-year history.

MICK BATES

Mick Bates was not an automatic first choice for Leeds United's first team during his twelve-year association with the club, but he fulfilled an essential role in Don Revie's legendary squad as they took on all-comers at home and abroad.

Born in Doncaster on 19 September 1947, after playing for Yorkshire Schools, Bates joined Leeds as an apprentice, signing professional forms in 1964. The Under-18 side was packed with talent when you consider his teammates included the likes of David Harvey, Peter Lorimer and Eddie Gray. With so much competition for places, patience was essential and Bates needed to have it because he had to wait until 1965/66 to make his first-team debut against Hartlepool in the League Cup.

Making 12 appearances the following term, it could not have been easy watching from the sidelines for long periods, but it did not help that he had to compete with Billy Bremner and Johnny Giles for a midfield berth. Nevertheless, whenever called upon, Bates, modest, compact and a fine passer of the ball, never let anyone down and was a valuable member of Revie's legendary squad.

Bates' role, like Rod Belfitt, Jimmy Greenhoff, Terry Hibbitt and eventually Terry Yorath was a testament to Revie's man-management skills because all could undoubtedly have been a regular for the majority of First Division teams. Revie, however, realised the importance of a big pool of players with his team battling on all fronts, and a player of Bates' calibre and loyalty was a vital element to his overall strategy. All stayed at least five years, Bates the longest, and would win more honours.

During his years at Leeds, Bates enjoyed extended first-team runs in 1970/71 and 1972/73, and in his 10 league appearances in 1973/74, he scored the only goal at Manchester City and a sweet strike against West Ham, which proved significant during a key stage of the Championship-winning campaign.

A member of both Fairs Cup-winning sides, the highlight of his career came in the first leg of the 1970/71 final against Juventus, when he scored a cracking equaliser in the 2-2 draw in Turin, which proved decisive as Leeds won the trophy on away goals. A non-playing substitute in two FA Cup finals, Bates' last appearance in a major final ended in heartbreak after Leeds' infamous European Cup Winners' Cup defeat to AC Milan in 1973.

At the end of the 1975/76 season Bates joined Walsall for £25,000, where he skippered the side during a two-year spell. In 1978 he joined Bradford City for £20,000 before playing briefly for Doncaster Rovers. Mick Bates may not have grabbed the headlines like many of his famous colleagues but his 151 (+36 substitute) appearances for Leeds were crucial and recognised by his colleagues and supporters alike during a glorious decade of success at Elland Road.

DAVID BATTY

David Batty epitomised the never-say-die attitude that Leeds United supporters admire about a footballer. Refusing to shirk a challenge, Batty's passion, tenacity and determination to fight for every ball made him indispensable, especially during the first of two spells at the club, when he was a key figure in the sides that claimed two Divisional titles.

Born in Leeds on 2 December 1968, Batty represented his city at every level, played for Yorkshire Schools and had trials for England before joining his hometown team as an apprentice. Playing regularly for the youth team, Billy Bremner gave his protégé a first-team debut against Preston North End in November 1987. Cementing his place as the midfield anchor, within months the youngster was an England Under-21 star.

When Howard Wilkinson became manager, Batty continued to progress. A key member of the 1989/90 Second Division title-winning squad, Batty was the club's Player of the Year the following term, and formed an integral part of the midfield quartet alongside Gordon Strachan, Gary McAllister and Gary Speed that was so influential during the club's First Division Championship success in 1991/92. Not renowned for his scoring ability, Batty thrilled fans with terrific strikes against Manchester City and Notts County during the campaign.

It seemed only a matter of time before this combative midfielder captained his boyhood team on a regular basis. However, to the horror of Leeds fans, Batty was allowed to join

David Batty in action against Everton.

Blackburn Rovers in October 1993 for £2.75m, where he helped Rovers clinch the Premier League in 1994/95. In 1996, Kevin Keegan took him to Newcastle United where he teamed up again with Speed. During a two-year spell, he helped the Geordies finish runners-up in both the Premier League and FA Cup.

Batty's roots, however, have always been in Leeds and when the opportunity of a return to Elland Road materialised in December 1998 he made a welcome return as David O'Leary's first signing for £4.4m. Unfortunately, an injury in his first game kept him sidelined for a season. However, by the end of 1999/2000 campaign Batty was back, adding solidity and experience to O'Leary's young team as they reached the semi-finals of the UEFA Cup and qualified for the Champions League for the first time. In 2000/01, after a further spell out through injury, he once again returned to play a key role as Leeds reached the semi-finals of Europe's premier competition and established themselves as a top Premiership side.

An England regular for many years, Batty won 42 caps during an impressive career that saw him play in the 1998 World Cup finals, which ended when he missed a penalty in a shoot-out defeat against Argentina. Despite not being a regular in the Leeds first team during recent seasons, David Batty's efforts in 350 (+22 substitute) games for Leeds United were exemplary.

Belfitt beats Ian Ure
to the ball in a
clash against
Manchester United.

Rod Belfitt was unable to command a regular place in Leeds United's first team throughout his eight years with the club; nevertheless, he fulfilled an important role in Don Revie's legendary squad.

Born in Doncaster, on 30 October 1945, Belfitt played for Doncaster United and Retford Town while training as a draughtsman, before joining Leeds as an apprentice in July 1963. A member of a fine Under-18 side that included the likes of David Harvey, Peter Lorimer and Eddie Gray, Belfitt was one of the first youngsters to break through to the first team as a replacement for Don Weston against Blackpool in September 1964.

Belfitt's first goal followed swiftly with the winner in a 3-2 League Cup victory against Huddersfield Town. Playing 9 games during the 1964/65 campaign, Belfitt scored an impressive 5 goals. Over the coming seasons though, with the arrival of Mick Jones in 1967 and Allan Clarke in 1970, Belfitt would rarely feature in First Division fixtures, starting 10 games in 1966/67 and 1971/72, and 11 in 1967/68.

ROD BELFITT

Belfitt scores against Sunderland in an FA Cup clash.

Cup competitions, however, would enable Belfitt to make his mark. After a European bow against Valencia in 1965/66, Belfitt featured prominently in the following term's Fairs Cup, notching his only Leeds hat-trick in a 4-2 aggregate win against Kilmarnock in the semi-finals. Reaching a first European final was a major triumph for Leeds despite a 2-0 defeat; Belfitt played in both legs against Dynamo Zagreb.

In 1967/68, after a number of near-misses, honours finally came to Elland Road. Belfitt missed only one tie in Leeds' march to the League Cup final, coming up trumps in the semi-final second leg against Derby County. Belfitt's brace ensured Leeds reached Wembley 4-3 on aggregate. Unlucky not to start the final against Arsenal, Belfitt made his only appearance at the Twin Towers as a second-half substitute for Gray. During four Fairs Cup appearances, Belfitt struck a crucial goal in a 3-2 win over Partizan Belgrade and came on as a substitute for Jones in the first leg of the final against Ferencvaros.

Belfitt's reliability was a tribute to his manager's man-management skills. Revie knew the importance of a big squad and Belfitt's calibre and loyalty was vital to his overall strategy. Although not dangerous aerially like Jones, Belfitt shielded the ball well, had a neat touch and his 33 goals proved important. In 8 league games during 1968/69, Belfitt scored 3 times, but all were in tight matches and gained valuable points in two hard-fought victories against Ipswich Town and a draw against Sunderland.

In November 1971, Belfitt decided to join Ipswich. Staying one year, he also played briefly for Everton, Sunderland, Fulham and Huddersfield Town prior to winding down his career at a number of non-league clubs. A fringe player maybe, Belfitt appeared 104 (+24 substitute) times for Leeds United, but his task was essential during the Revie era. A member of the squads that won the League Cup and Fairs Cup, Rod Belfitt was a fine player for the club.

WILLIE BELL

Willie Bell was an integral part of Leeds United's defence as Don Revie's team developed into a formidable outfit in the mid-1960s. Originally a tough-tackling midfield player, Bell converted to left-back with great success.

Born in Lanarkshire on 3 September 1937, Bell joined Queens Park in 1957 where he impressed in the centre of the park. Following his Leeds debut in 1960 against Leyton Orient, Bell notched his first goal for the club against Lincoln City in a 7-0 win before eventually succeeding stalwart defender Grenville Hair in 1963/64 as Leeds won promotion to the First Division.

Bell grabbed two goals during the campaign, Leeds' winner in a 2-1 win against Swansea Town and a thirty-yard screamer against Plymouth Argyle in the penultimate game of the season. Despite lacking natural pace, over the coming season, as Leeds finished runners-up in both the League and FA Cup, Bell utilised his anticipation, determination and tackling ability to become a solid defender alongside Paul Reaney, Jack Charlton and Norman Hunter.

Although not a classy player, the popular Scot developed a tremendous understanding with flying winger Albert Johannesson down the left flank. Bell also scored some crucial goals, one of the most infamous against Everton in a notorious encounter at Goodison Park in November 1964, which Leeds won 1-0. Not only did Everton have Sandy Brown sent off after just two minutes for hacking Bell down, but both teams were ordered off the pitch by the referee to calm down! In 1966/67, Bell played against Dynamo Zagreb in the club's first Fairs Cup final and his form deservedly won him, somewhat belatedly in his career, 2 caps for Scotland.

When the 1967/68 campaign began Bell realised that he had serious competition for his place with the emergence of Terry Cooper, who had started out on the left wing before being converted to left-back under Revie's watchful eye. Within a few games, it was apparent that Bell would no longer be first choice so it came as no surprise when he joined Leicester City for £40,000 after a tremendous career which had seen him play 260 games, scoring 18 goals, for Leeds.

At Leicester, Bell became skipper but an injury meant that he missed much of the 1968/69 campaign when City suffered relegation and reached an FA Cup final. During the close season, Bell moved to Brighton & Hove Albion where he ended his playing days. Following his retirement Bell took up a coaching post at Birmingham City alongside ex-Leeds teammate Freddie Goodwin, before taking the helm as manager for two years in the mid-1970s. Subsequently he had a brief spell as manager of Lincoln City.

Willie Bell achieved his potential during his years at Leeds United. A talented footballer, Bell was one of a number of players who paved the way for the glory years under Revie.

LEE BOWYER

Lee Bowyer became British football's most expensive teenage transfer when he joined Leeds United for £1.5m from Charlton Athletic in 1996. A ball-winner one moment and goalscorer the next, Bowyer covered every blade of grass for the benefit of his team.

Born in London on 3 January 1977, Bowyer was Howard Wilkinson's last signing for Leeds and made a scoring debut against Derby County on the opening day of the 1996/97 season. Leeds fans loved his all-action style, despite the occasional absence due to suspension following over-exuberance in his tackling and discipline on the pitch.

Under new boss George Graham, Bowyer progressed even though Leeds spent the season grinding out results. When Graham signed David Hopkin, Bowyer found himself out of favour but, rather than bemoan his bad luck, forced his way into the starting line-up with sterling performances, none better than when he sent Elland Road wild with a last-minute winner against Derby as Leeds overturned a three-goal deficit to win a classic match 4-3.

When David O'Leary took the helm in 1998/99, Bowyer excelled as Leeds qualified for Europe. Finishing second-top scorer with Alan Smith and Harry Kewell, Bowyer scored fine goals in both fixtures against West Ham. With David Batty and Eirik Bakke's arrival, Bowyer supported the strikers superbly and enjoyed his most prolific season in 1999/2000, scoring 11 goals as Leeds qualified for the Champions League and reached the semi-finals of the UEFA Cup. Among notable goals were terrific strikes against Newcastle United and Slavia Prague.

In 2000/01, despite off-the-field distractions that would hamper most players, Bowyer played superbly. His goals, and performances in the Champions League, were key factors in Leeds reaching the semi-finals and his controversial absence in the second leg against Valencia was a major factor in the side's subsequent elimination from Europe's premier competition.

The coming two seasons, however, would see Bowyer's relationship with the club and supporters sour dramatically in the aftermath of his much-publicised court case alongside Jonathan Woodgate. Amidst unprecedented media frenzy, a loss of form followed and the eventual breakdown of a proposed move to Liverpool cost the club millions. In the end, it was a relief when Bowyer joined West Ham United after 257 (+8 substitute) appearances for a nominal fee. Following the Hammers' relegation to Division One in 2002/03, Bowyer joined Newcastle United but has only recently featured in the first team.

It has been a sad demise for a player who appeared to have the football world at his feet. Voted the club's Player of the Year in 1998/99 and 2000/01, only time will tell whether this former England international can rediscover the form that made him an essential member of David O'Leary's midfield as Leeds thrilled supporters at home and in Europe.

Billy Bremner is the greatest player to represent Leeds United. His never-say-die attitude, playing ability and inspirational leadership drove the team forward throughout the Don Revie era; taking the club from Second Division minnows to one of European football's most respected and feared outfits.

Born in Stirling on 9 December 1942, Bremner was considered too small by Arsenal and Chelsea. Joining Leeds at seventeen, he made his debut in January 1960 against Chelsea; one of his teammates was Don Revie before his appointment as manager. Despite early setbacks due to homesickness, his playing career at Elland Road would span sixteen years.

Revie recognised the raw talent Bremner possessed, even though his fiery temperament resulted in a number of brushes with the Football Association. Throughout Bremner's career his desire to win never diminished. A classic picture with Dave Mackay summed up his attitude following an incident at White Hart Lane in the mid-1960s. Mackay does not look amused following the clash!

Playing alongside future skipper Bobby Collins and Jack Charlton in 1961/62, Leeds escaped relegation when Third Division football seemed inevitable, and with the introduction of youngsters such as Gary Sprake, Paul Reaney and Norman Hunter, Leeds improved rapidly, clinching the Second Division title in 1963/64; their first divisional success for forty years.

Billy Bremner gets his hands on the
FA Cup.

Bremner shows fans the Fairs
Cup after defeating Ferencvaros.

Taking the First Division by storm, Leeds astounded everyone by finishing runners-up in both the League and FA Cup. Though heartbreaking, supporters will never forget Bremner's winner in the dying minutes of the cup semi-final against Manchester United and even though Liverpool edged the Wembley final, Bremner scored a scorcher as an exciting era dawned.

The 1965/66 campaign saw Bremner appointed captain following a long-term injury to Collins in a Fairs Cup clash, and under his leadership Leeds claimed the First Division title and Fairs Cup twice, the FA Cup, League Cup and Charity Shield. In addition, Revie's team finished First Division runners-up five times, lost three FA Cup finals and two European finals. Bremner missed the European Cup Winners' Cup final defeat due to suspension. Although many honours eluded Leeds, the team's consistency was unrivalled for a decade.

One of the most recognised footballers of his era, Bremner was voted Footballer of the Year in 1969/70. Having represented Scotland at Schoolboy and Under-23 level, he made his full Scottish debut against Spain in 1965. Acknowledged as world class, Bremner faced all the legendary players of world football. Winning 54 caps, many as captain, Bremner's finest moment came when he led Scotland in the 1974 World Cup finals. Arguably, however, the most famous game he played for his country was when Scotland defeated England 3-2 at Wembley to become the first team to defeat the 1966 World Cup winners.

As a player he had everything. Strength, stamina, fine passing and shooting ability, and brilliant anticipation. Bremner was a ball-winner one moment, a goalscorer the next. At times for Leeds he also excelled as an emergency defender, striker or sweeper but it was in midfield, in tandem with Johnny Giles that he made his mark. Bremner and Giles complemented each other perfectly, becoming the most feared midfield partnership at home and in Europe.

For a midfield player, Bremner's haul of 115 goals was an incredible achievement and many of them were crucial. Three in FA Cup semi-finals took Leeds to Wembley and his flying header at Liverpool won a classic Fairs Cup semi-final clash in 1971. On five occasions Bremner hit double figures during a season. The last, in 1973/74, was particularly special, as many pundits had written Revie's team off following the cup final disappointments the previous season. As an unbeaten run of 29 games engineered a second Championship the diminutive Scot scored 10 goals, including two in the run-in against Derby and Ipswich, which proved vital.

Following Don Revie's departure to become England manager it was only a matter of time before Bremner moved on. There would be one more Wembley appearance in the Charity Shield when he was sensationally sent off for fighting with Kevin Keegan, before a final tilt at the European Cup. During a memorable campaign, Bremner scored a tremendous goal against Barcelona in the semi-final, before the ultimate prize was snatched from his grasp in the final after some dubious refereeing decisions.

Bremner made his last appearance for Leeds at Elland Road in a 2-2 draw with Newcastle United in September 1976, taking his total number of appearances to 772 (+1 substitute), a record he shares with Jack Charlton, before joining Hull City for £35,000. His transfer was a major coup for the Tigers and helped swell attendances, but he wanted to become a manager and got his chance with Doncaster Rovers in 1978. After a handful of games, he finally retired as a player and guided Rovers twice to promotion. In October 1985, he replaced Eddie Gray at his beloved Leeds United.

Languishing in the Second Division, despite limited funds, Bremner threw himself into the job and by the start of the 1986/87 season had rebuilt the team around Mervyn Day, John Sheridan and Ian Baird. With self-belief among his players increasing throughout a memorable campaign, his endeavours to guide Leeds back into the big time appeared on track as Leeds battled to the semi-finals of the FA Cup and the Second Division play-off final.

Heartbreakingly, Leeds failed when success appeared within reach, losing to Coventry City in a classic semi-final. Even more dramatically, Charlton Athletic overturned a Sheridan strike in the last seven minutes to deny a Leeds return to top-flight football. It was a crushing end to a pulsating campaign.

After the dust had settled, Bremner's reward was an extended contract, but the players failed to deliver in 1987/88 and after making a poor start the following term his association with Leeds United ended in October 1988. Bremner's tenure may have finished but his presence had brought renewed hope for long-suffering supporters. Following a two-year spell with Doncaster Rovers, Bremner began a career as an accomplished after-dinner speaker until his sudden death in 1997, aged 54.

Today, a statue of Billy Bremner greets supporters to Elland Road, a reminder of the fighting spirit he displayed endlessly for the club. King Billy is the most successful captain in Leeds United's history. A legend, his achievements will never be forgotten.

TOMMY BURDEN

Tommy Burden joined Leeds United in July 1948 from Chester. It was a period of great change at Elland Road as Major Frank Buckley began replacing players whose careers had ended during the Second World War. Burden would become a stalwart of the team.

Born in Andover, 21 February 1924, Burden represented Somerset county boys and came to the attention of Buckley during the hostilities when, aged sixteen, he played for Wolves, managed by Buckley at the time. Serving the Rifle Brigade and Royal Fusiliers, Burden was wounded during the D-Day landings. Regaining full fitness, Buckley signed Burden for Leeds after he impressed his former boss while playing for the Third Division (North) club.

Buckley was trying to build a team capable of winning back their First Division status following relegation to the Second Division in 1946/47; the first season of professional football after the war. Seen as an ideal addition to the likes of Jim Milburn, Jimmy Dunn, Jim McCabe and David Cochrane, Burden quickly settled at Elland Road, even though it was a step up in class.

A tough-tackling wing half, Burden made his first-team debut at Sheffield Wednesday in September 1948 and quickly displayed his leadership skills. Shrewd, confident and a good team player, Burden's consistent performances were rewarded when he was made team captain; a position he held for four seasons, even though he continued to live in the West Country. Unbeknown to the skipper, as a goalscorer he was something of a lucky mascot because after scoring twice in a 6-3 win over Grimsby in 1948 Leeds would only lose once when he scored one of his 'unlucky' 13!

The 1949/50 campaign was Burden's first full season at the club. Enjoying their best campaign for many seasons, Burden scored 6 goals, including a brace in a 2-1 win at Leicester City as Leeds won six of their final seven league games to finish fifth. They also reached the quarter-finals of the FA Cup for the first time. The run ended at Arsenal, the eventual winners of the trophy that term, but the players' escapades generated genuine 'cup fever' for supporters in the city.

During his tenure as skipper, Leeds were a solid outfit, never finishing out of the top ten, but they were not clinical enough to make a concerted promotion challenge. By 1953/54, Raich Carter had replaced Buckley as manager, and it would be Burden's final campaign at Leeds. After six seasons of dedicated service, Burden requested a transfer to enable him to move back closer to his home and the Leeds board granted his wish.

Joining Bristol City in October 1954, Burden helped City win the Third Division (South) title in 1954/55. His old team, within a season, was back at Elland Road, and Tommy Burden, who made 259 appearances, had played his part.

RAICH CARTER

April 1957. Carter watches Bolton (chairman) shake hands with Charles before John's last game at Elland Road in League football.

Raich Carter took the helm at Leeds United during the 1953/54 close season, succeeding Major Frank Buckley. During a five-year spell, Carter guided Leeds to promotion in a memorable campaign in 1955/56.

Born in Hendon, Sunderland, 21 December 1913, 'Horatio' Carter was a schoolboy international and signed as a professional for his hometown club in 1931, heralding a glorious career at Sunderland and Derby County. The youngest skipper of a First Division-winning team in 1935/36, Carter won an FA Cup winners medal with Sunderland the following term. A star in wartime internationals alongside Stanley Matthews, Carter gained 13 England caps and helped Derby County win the FA Cup in 1947.

A county cricketer with Derbyshire, Carter became player-manager at Hull City in 1948, replacing Major Buckley. Buying and selling Don Revie, Carter guided the Tigers to the Third Division (North) title in 1949, ending his playing career with 218 goals from 451 games. Retiring in 1951 to run a sweet shop, Carter helped Hull briefly as they battled relegation, prior to guiding Cork Athletic to the 1953 FA of Ireland Cup final. His experience brought him to the attention of Leeds United.

Altering little, Carter kept faith with the backbone of Buckley's team with seven players; Jimmy Dunn, Grenville Hair, Eric Kerfoot, Tommy Burden, Harold Williams, Albert Nightingale and John Charles featuring in at least thirty-seven league games. Leeds got off to a flyer with Charles scoring seven goals in two opening victories! Notching five hat-tricks, Charles scored 42 goals, which is still a club record.

Unfortunately, Carter had a major dilemma because, for all Charles' prowess as a striker, the defence leaked 81 goals, nullifying the 89 goals scored. Finishing tenth, Carter signed Harold Brook and controversially moved Charles back to centre half in a bid to shore up the defence. To Carter's credit, Brook finished the season top scorer and Leeds overcame four defeats in the opening five fixtures to miss promotion by just one point, ending the 1954/55 campaign in fourth place.

Raich Carter,
extreme right.

The campaign had seen the introduction of Roy Wood in goal, and expectations for a promotion charge were high within the club, but Leeds stuttered. Struggling for goals, Carter signed Jack Overfield and switched Charles to centre forward, drafting in the inexperienced Jack Charlton at centre half. Charles immediately hit a rich vein of form but Leeds were a long way off the pace. Few pundits backed Leeds for promotion because they were still inconsistent.

Suddenly during the run-in, Carter's team hit an amazing vein of form, winning their last six matches, Charles scoring nine goals, to snatch the runners-up spot behind Sheffield Wednesday. It was exceedingly close; indeed, Leeds only controlled their destiny after coming from behind to defeat arch-rivals Bristol Rovers 2-1 in the last home game, before sealing promotion with a 2-0 win at Rotherham United prior to a 4-1 victory at Carter's former club Hull City on the last day of the season.

Back in the First Division, Leeds began with a 5-1 win against Everton. With Charles in imperious form, scoring 38 goals, Leeds finished eighth, but Carter could no longer hang on to his star player as offers flooded in. Unable to utilise a large proportion of the £65,000 generated from Charles' sale due to the building of a new stand destroyed by fire in September 1956, Leeds struggled and did well to survive in 1957/58. However, it was still somewhat surprising when the Leeds board decided not to renew his contract at the end of the campaign.

Carter was soon in demand though. Guiding Mansfield to promotion from the Fourth Division in 1962/63, he managed Middlesbrough for three years before retiring from the game in 1966. Throughout his years in football, Raich Carter, who died in 1994, was one of the most popular personalities in the game. An exceptional footballer, as a manager Carter's greatest success was at Leeds United, bringing top-flight football to Elland Road after a nine-year absence.

ERIC CANTONA

Eric Cantona joined Leeds United in February 1992, adding depth to Howard Wilkinson's squad and momentum to the team's title aspirations. Though his stay would be brief, Cantona left his mark.

Born in Paris, 24 May 1966, Cantona's arrival at Leeds followed spells at Auxerre, Marseille, Bordeaux, Montpellier, where he won the French Cup, and Nimes. Possessing undoubted skills, Cantona made headlines for the wrong reasons. In 1991, Nimes cancelled his contract after he threw a ball at a referee and walked off the pitch. His troubles extended to the international stage. Having played for the French Youth and Under-21 teams, Cantona made his full debut against West Germany in 1987 but within twelve months had received a year's international ban following a disagreement with the team manager.

Cantona announced his retirement following a disciplinary hearing at Nimes but suddenly reappeared at Sheffield Wednesday for trials. As Wednesday considered their position, Wilkinson snapped him up on a loan deal to the end of the 1991/92 season. Many observers perceived Cantona's arrival at Elland Road as a gamble; the mercurial Frenchman was a genius, but could the Leeds boss handle him?

Leeds supporters greeted Cantona enthusiastically as the team battled for the title with Manchester United. Following a media frenzy on his debut at Oldham Athletic, Cantona started six games and displayed his rich array of skills. A powerful runner, Cantona controlled a ball in an instant and could deliver the most sublime flicks, back-heels and passes. Dazzling supporters at times, his wonder-goal against Chelsea during the run-in was one of the

Cantona cracks in a classy goal at Wembley.

Liverpool are helpless to prevent Eric Cantona scoring with a header to complete a fine hat-trick in Leeds Charity Shield victory.

highlights of the season as Leeds marched to the title. Leeds fans had a new hero and Wilkinson wasted no time in securing his services in a £900,000 deal.

When the 1992/93 season began, Cantona was in the starting eleven and joined an elite band of players to score a hat-trick at Wembley with a magnificent treble in Leeds' 4-3 victory over Liverpool in the Charity Shield. In so doing, he became the only player in the club's history to score a hat-trick at the famous stadium. The Twin Towers rocked to 'Ooh-ah Cantona!'

Cantona began the league campaign brilliantly, scoring six goals in the opening seven games, including a treble against Tottenham, but his relationship with Wilkinson soon deteriorated. After a number of poor performances, Cantona stormed off when dropped prior to a clash with Arsenal. Within days of Leeds' 3-0 win Cantona joined Manchester United after just 25 (+10 substitute) appearances and 14 goals, for £1.2m. His transfer to the club's arch-rivals for what would prove to be a pittance angered supporters.

The central figure in the Old Trafford club's domination of the Premier League during the remainder of the decade, despite several controversial incidents, including a 'kung-fu' kick at Crystal Palace in 1995, among many honours, Cantona won the PFA and Football Writers' Player of the Year awards.

Cantona had panache, bundles of talent and many a time supporters would gasp at his undoubted brilliance. Sadly, for Leeds fans, the *enfant terrible* only demonstrated fleeting moments of his genius, notably his historic performance at Wembley in 1992.

HERBERT CHAPMAN

Herbert Chapman was Leeds City manager for seven years and at the helm when the Football League expelled City in 1919 after allegedly making illegal payments to players. Successfully appealing against his suspension, Chapman became one of the greatest managers of all time at Huddersfield Town and Arsenal.

Born in Sheffield, 19 January 1878, Chapman played for a number of clubs, including Stalybridge, Rochdale, Grimsby and Worksop at inside forward while pursuing a career as a mining engineer, before signing professional forms with Northampton, which is where he was offered his first managerial post in 1907.

Tactically astute, charismatic, a great motivator and innovative, Chapman guided his charges to the Southern League title in 1908/09. His success brought him to the attention of Leeds City, who appointed him manager-secretary in 1912 as replacement for Frank Scott-Walford after City finished bottom of the table.

Successfully campaigning for Leeds' re-election to the Football League, Chapman set about developing his team. Quickly realising the key to success was to get the best out of star striker Billy McLeod, during his first season at the helm Chapman signed inside left James Spiers, who led Bradford City to an FA Cup triumph in 1911, and outside right Simpson Bainbridge. With additional support for outside left Fred Croot results improved. Finishing sixth, McLeod grabbed 27 league goals, 13 more than he accrued the previous season.

With 'keeper Tony Hogg settling into the side and defender George Affleck back from injury the defence was settled. McLeod was firing on all cylinders and the team got off to a fine start. By the end of the campaign, McLeod had equalled his previous season's total, and City were somewhat unlucky to miss promotion to the First Division by just 2 points. Looking back on the campaign, four defeats at the turn of the year cost City dear. Finishing fourth would be City's highest ever finish.

Leeds City A.F.C Team 1912-13. Back row: A.J. Murrell (Trainer), A. Stead (Assistant Trainer), Mr J. Whitman, J. Robertson, G. Law, A. Roberts, W. Scott, A. Hogg, T.H. Moran, W. McLeod, J.W. Stead, Mr C. Hepworth, Mr H. Chapman. Middle row: R. Roberts, H. Bridgett, J. Enright, A.Gibson, H.P. Roberts, J. Allan, M. Foley, F. Croot. Front row: G. Cunningham, J. Ferguson, L. Johnson, S. Cubberley, G. Affleck.

HERBERT CHAPMAN

The final campaign before the First World War was an anti-climax as City finished fifteenth, but during the war years Chapman continued to manage City and they were tremendously successful in Midland Section tournaments, when more than thirty guest players, including many internationals starred.

Twice winners of the Principal Tournament, City won the Subsidiary Tournament (Northern Division) and League Championship play-off against Stoke in 1917/18. However, following the hostilities, after winning four of their opening eight games, club administrators refused to present official books for examination, which resulted in the club losing its League status.

Chapman quit the game in December 1919, believing the FA Commission had harshly treated him. Manager at a munitions factory during the war, he claimed that he was not in the office when the alleged payments occurred. Suspended for a short time, Chapman was eventually exonerated. Working as an industrial manager in Selby, Chapman returned to football at Huddersfield Town in 1921.

Chapman was a revelation. Guiding Huddersfield to the FA Cup in 1922 and the First Division title twice, he repeated the successes at Arsenal, winning the FA Cup in 1930 and First Division titles in 1930/31 and 1932/33. Tragically, Herbert Chapman died after contracting pneumonia following a scouting trip in 1934 and football mourned the loss of a legendary character. Historically, Leeds City supporters could only speculate what might have been but for the illegal payments scandal.

LEE CHAPMAN

Chapman celebrates after scoring against West Ham.

Lee Chapman was an archetypal centre forward who led the line for Leeds United superbly during their title triumphs of the early 1990s. His prowess made him the most successful striker at the club since the Don Revie era.

Born in Lincoln, 5 December 1959, the son of former Aston Villa star Roy Chapman, Lee made his debut for Stoke City in 1978, striking a hat-trick against Leeds in February 1981. He went on to experience mixed fortunes at Plymouth Argyle, Arsenal, Sunderland, Sheffield Wednesday (managed by Howard Wilkinson), and Nottingham Forest; where he played in two Wembley triumphs in 1988/89.

Replacing Ian Baird in attack, not everyone acclaimed his £400,000 transfer to Elland Road in January 1989, but Chapman quickly became the final piece of Wilkinson's team challenging for promotion. Scoring on his league debut at Blackburn Rovers, Chapman partnered Bobby Davison, Carl Shutt and Imre Varadi and went on to score 12 goals during the run-in, which proved a significant factor in Leeds winning promotion instead of drifting into the play-offs. To complete a memorable season his bullet header at Bournemouth clinched the title and a return to the First Division after eight years in the wilderness.

Top scorer during the 1990/91 campaign with 31 goals, the highest total by any player in the First Division that term and the most by a Leeds player since the days of John Charles, his contribution to Wilkinson's side cannot be underestimated. Although susceptible to missing the occasional sitter, Chapman could not stop scoring goals in all four competitions Leeds entered, grabbing a brace against Norwich City, Chelsea, Sunderland, Aston Villa, Nottingham Forest and Everton. The prolific striker also notched his first Leeds hat-trick in an astonishing 5-4 defeat at home to Liverpool.

In 1991/92, Chapman's presence would prove invaluable throughout the campaign as the team battled for the title with Manchester United. Not only did he finish the season as the

Chapman scores against Wimbledon during the 1991/92 championship winning campaign.

club's top scorer once again, his very presence unnerved opponents, allowing space for other players to strike.

Chapman may have lacked genuine pace but nobody could doubt his power in the air, bravery and ability to lead the line. He also forged a great understanding alongside Rod Wallace, Carl Shutt and Eric Cantona. During a memorable campaign Chapman grabbed hat-tricks against Sheffield Wednesday and Wimbledon and scored a number of outstanding goals; none better than his flying header in a 4-1 win at Aston Villa.

Although Chapman helped Leeds win the Charity Shield at Wembley and was top scorer for a third successive season in 1992/93, the first player to achieve the feat since Arthur Hydes (1933-35), it was clear that his days at Leeds were numbered with the impending arrival of Sheffield United's Brian Deane.

Before the start of the new campaign, he joined Portsmouth for £250,000 but his stay at the South Coast club would last a handful of games as an opportunity to return to the Premier League materialised. For three seasons, West Ham and Ipswich Town benefited before his days as a striker ended at Southend, Swansea City and a two-game return to Leeds during an injury crisis at Elland Road in 1996.

Chapman scored over 200 goals during an eighteen-year career, but at Leeds United he enjoyed his most consistent form, notching 80 goals in 171 (+4 substitute) appearances, which was rewarded with an England 'B' appearance. One of only four players alongside Tom Jennings, John Charles and Peter Lorimer to score 30 goals in a season, Lee Chapman is the club's most potent striker of the last three decades.

JOHN CHARLES

John Charles is the greatest 'all-round' footballer Britain has produced. World class at both centre half and centre forward, Charles was the star attraction at Leeds United during the 1950s.

Born 27 December 1931, Charles was playing for a Swansea schools' team when spotted by Leeds scouts in South Wales. It is quite astonishing that his local club Swansea Town had not snapped him up, but following his arrival at Elland Road, the teenager made an immediate impression following his league debut at the age of seventeen at Blackburn Rovers in April 1949.

Welsh international selectors had also taken note and within a year made him the youngest player to win full international honours for his country. Charles eventually won 38 caps, scoring 15 goals, but would be best remembered for his displays during the 1958 World Cup finals when Wales reached the quarter-finals before falling to eventual winners Brazil.

Initially, Charles played at centre half for Leeds as Major Frank Buckley rebuilt the team following the club's relegation to the Second Division in 1946/47. The 1949/50 campaign, Charles' first full season in the side, saw Leeds finishing fifth and reach the FA Cup quarter-finals for the first time in the club's history. Charles made his mark as a formidable opponent. Few opponents got the better of him and always knew they would be in for a difficult game. They were never disappointed!

A few months into the 1952/53 season, Charles moved to centre forward due to a lack of firepower with stunning effect. Scoring 11 goals in his opening 8 games as a striker, Charles finished the season top scorer with 26 goals from 28 games, including three hat-tricks!

A complete natural, during the 1953/54 campaign Charles scored 42 goals, the best return to date by any Leeds United player. During a season of records, Charles scored 15 goals in the opening 10 games, and hit a club-record five hat-tricks against Notts County (four goals), Rotherham United (home and away), Bury and Lincoln City. This extraordinary player is still one of only two players, along with Charlie Keetley, to score three hat-tricks for Leeds in a season.

With clubs around the country aware of his talent, new boss Raich Carter had a dilemma because for all Charles' success in attack, the defence was leaking goals. During the previous season, Leeds scored 89 goals but let in 81. Carter's answer was to sign Harold Brook and controversially move Charles back to defence. To Carter's credit, Leeds ended the 1954/55 campaign in fourth place, missing promotion by a single point, but Charles was restless for top-flight football and handed in a transfer request during the season. Although the Leeds board turned the request down they realised he could not be held back much longer.

Expectations were high for a promotion charge but Leeds stuttered. Struggling for goals, Carter switched Charles to centre forward again and brought the inexperienced Jack Charlton in at centre half. Charles immediately hit a rich vein of form; scoring 9 goals in 6 games. By the end of the season, 28 of his league goals had come in as many games. Even so, few pundits would have backed Leeds for promotion because they were still inconsistent. Astonishingly with nine games remaining they hit a purple patch, winning eight (Charles scoring 12 goals), to snatch the runners-up spot behind Sheffield Wednesday.

It had been incredibly close and there were two crucial games. First was the last home game of the season against promotion rivals Bristol Rovers when Charles equalised as Leeds came from behind to win 2-1, placing them second for the first time. Then, following a midweek win at Rotherham, Leeds went into their last match at Hull City knowing a win would seal promotion. Charles grabbed two goals in a 4-1 win.

Nine years after being relegated Leeds were back in the First Division and Charles could test himself against the likes of Harry Johnson, Duncan Edwards and Billy Wright. In his debut season he scored in an opening day 5-1 win against Everton and by the finish had top scored for the fourth time in five campaigns with 38 goals, including a hat-trick both home and away against Sheffield Wednesday. His two trebles took Charles' total of hat-tricks to 11, the highest number by any Leeds United player.

In his final game for Leeds at Elland Road in April 1957, and last game of a memorable season, Charles grabbed two goals in a 3-1 win against a Sunderland team captained by Don

In the last home game of the 1955/56 season, before an ecstatic crowd of over 49,000, John Charles scores the opening goal.

Rotherham goalkeeper Reg Quairney gathers a cross before Charles can pounce in the penultimate match of the promotion campaign.

Revie. Leeds ended the campaign in eighth place and Charles' days at the club were over as offers flooded in. The Leeds board could no longer hang on to their prize asset and accepted a world-record bid of £65,000 from Italian giants Juventus, using the money to rebuild the West Stand destroyed by a fire that season.

Dubbed the 'Gentle Giant' in Italy, Charles quickly became the star attraction. During a five-year spell in Turin, he gained three championship medals, an Italian Cup winner's medal and was Footballer of the Year. Recently, Charles was nominated as the greatest foreign player ever to wear the club's world-renowned shirt; an astonishing accolade when you consider the talent that has represented this famous club.

Don Revie brought Charles back to Leeds in 1962 but his stay was brief and he soon returned to Italy to play for AS Roma. Before hanging up his boots, he played two seasons with Cardiff City before taking on managerial and coaching posts with Hereford, Swansea City and Merthyr Tydfil.

Until his death earlier this year, Charles was a regular at Elland Road. Instantly recognisable, those who witnessed this footballing legend play believe he is the finest player in the club's history. Top scorer on four occasions, one of only four in the club's history, this colossus of a footballer scored 157 goals in 327 games for Leeds United, is the only player to score 40 goals in a season and the second-highest goalscorer in the club's history. King John received the CBE in 2001 and his memory will last forever.

JACK CHARLTON ——————————

Jack Charlton is one of Leeds United's greatest ever servants. Big Jack was a member of a remarkable footballing family. Elder brother to Manchester United and England legend Bobby, three of his uncles, George, Jim and Jack Milburn all served Leeds with distinction. Indeed, Jim recommended his nephew while he was playing at Elland Road.

Born in Ashington, on 25 April 1935, Charlton joined Leeds as an amateur in 1950 before signing professional forms in 1952. Following his debut against Doncaster Rovers on the last day of the 1952/53 season, the lanky defender had to wait until the 1955/56 campaign to receive an extended run in the first team. Raich Carter was manager and with Leeds struggling for goals, Carter switched John Charles to centre forward and brought the inexperienced Charlton in at centre half.

Few pundits backed Leeds for promotion due to their inconsistency but eight wins in their last nine games snatched the runners-up spot behind Sheffield Wednesday. It had been mighty close though and, but for a 4-1 victory at Hull City in the last game of the season Leeds would have missed out.

Charlton's progress earned the first of six appearances for the Football League in 1957. However, with John Charles now at Juventus, playing in a struggling side hindered his development. It didn't help matters that his stubborn nature and strongly held views made for an uneasy relationship with management; nevertheless new boss Don Revie believed in his ability and began to get the best out of him.

Astonishingly, Charlton filled in as an emergency centre forward for a couple of seasons as Revie grappled with an injury crisis among his strikers and he never let his boss down, top scoring with 12 goals alongside Billy Bremner in 1961/62 as relegation to the Third Division was just averted! Centre of defence, though, was where Charlton would make his name.

With the introduction of Bobby Collins and youngsters Gary Sprake, Paul Reaney and Norman Hunter, Leeds improved rapidly, clinching the Second Division title in 1963/64; their first divisional success for forty years. A key member of the side, Charlton's performances the following term when Leeds came close to a League and FA Cup double finally won him England recognition when he made his full international debut against Scotland. Just over a year later, he formed a crucial partnership alongside skipper Bobby Moore in England's 1966 World Cup-winning team and eventually won 35 caps for his country.

Although assured on the field Charlton was superstitious and relinquished the Leeds captaincy because of his liking to leave the dressing room last! Although not the most stylish of defenders, Big Jack would crane his neck to dominate in the air and used his long stride to make telescopic tackles; attributes that saw him dubbed 'the giraffe'. His consistent performances brought him the 1967 Footballer of the Year award.

In every game opposing forwards knew they would face a stern task and opposing goalkeepers and defenders also feared him, especially at set pieces, because he caused havoc when standing

JACK CHARLTON

Charlton in action
against Juventus.

on their goal line. The number of goals he scored for a defender was phenomenal, 95 in all competitions. Notching his first against Blackburn Rovers in April 1959, many of Charlton's goals came from his tremendous heading ability, including a brace against Napoli in 1966 and the winner against Tottenham Hotspur in an FA Cup sixth-round clash in 1972.

After numerous near misses, Charlton claimed League Cup, First Division, FA Cup and Fairs Cup winners medals, and also appeared in two FA Cup finals and a Fairs Cup final during Leeds' rise to prominence. Twelve months after Leeds' FA Cup success time finally caught up with this football legend and he retired as a player at the end of the 1972/73 season aged thirty-eight. With George and Jack Milburn arriving at the club in 1928 the link between the Milburn family and Leeds United lasted forty-five years.

It was time for a new challenge and beginning his managerial career at Middlesbrough, Charlton made an immediate impact, winning the Manager of the Year award in 1973/74 after guiding his charges to the Second Division title. He enjoyed a successful spell at Sheffield Wednesday but a move to Newcastle United didn't work out. However, another challenge was soon on the horizon. Many pundits felt Charlton should have managed England, but the Football Association's loss was the Republic of Ireland's gain.

The role on the international stage was perfect for his style of management and during his tenure, Charlton guided the Republic to the 1988 European Championships; where they defeated England, the 1990 World Cup, where they reached the quarter-finals and the 1994 World Cup finals. After failing to guide the Republic to the 1996 European Championship finals, Charlton retired but was awarded the Freedom of Dublin.

In recent years, Jack Charlton has built a career as one of the most sought-after speakers at sporting dinners. A natural, his wit and wide range of anecdotal stories from four decades in the game makes for compulsive listening. However, Leeds United supporters remember him for his deeds during the Revie era when he helped Leeds take on all-comers at home and abroad. A one-club player, Charlton played more league matches than any other Leeds United player (628), and his 773 appearances in all competitions is a feat matched only by Billy Bremner. In a career that spanned twenty-one years, Big Jack was a true legend in every sense of the word.

TREVOR CHERRY

Trevor Cherry experienced the highs and lows of playing for Leeds United during a decade of dedicated service. From Championships to relegation, Cherry witnessed it all.

Born in Huddersfield, on 23 February 1948, Cherry led his hometown club to the Second Division title in 1968/69 before moving to Elland Road for £100,000 during the 1972/73 close season. Signed initially as a replacement for Terry Cooper, who broke his leg shortly before the 1972 FA Cup final, Cherry made his debut in the opening game of the new campaign at Chelsea and quickly cemented his place in the first team.

During his first two seasons, Cherry played in both the FA Cup and European Cup Winners' Cup final and was a member of Leeds' 1973/74 title-winning team. Following Revie's departure the following term, after scoring against Liverpool in the Charity Shield at Wembley, Cherry was in and out of the side under new bosses Brian Clough and Jimmy Armfield, though he was a member of the European Cup final squad.

A tough-tackling defender, Cherry possessed pace, determination, a calm temperament and supported the attack well. However, life was very different at Leeds as the likes of Billy Bremner, Norman Hunter and Johnny Giles moved on. In 1975/76, with Gordon McQueen sidelined for much of the season, Cherry proved his versatility. Comfortable in defence or midfield, at various times he filled in at right-back, centre-back and in midfield, and this flexibility would continue throughout his Leeds career. Following Bremner's departure, Cherry became captain and held the honour until his departure in 1982.

A regular during a difficult transitional period, Cherry experienced many changes at Elland Road and served seven managers. Following Revie, Clough and Armfield, Cherry worked under Jock Stein, Jimmy Adamson, Allan Clarke and Eddie Gray. Despite the upheaval, apart from a few months of the 1982/83 season, Cherry played for Leeds in the First Division and the team produced entertaining football, especially with the likes of Tony Currie and Arthur Graham in the side.

Don Revie gives Cherry a tour of Elland Road on his first day.

Cherry crashes home a goal against Ipswich Town.

Indeed, during the late 1970s Leeds were somewhat unlucky not to win any silverware; falling at the semi-final stage of both the FA Cup and League Cup. It was during the FA Cup run in 1977 that Cherry scored his most memorable goal for the club, in an unforgettable fifth-round encounter against Manchester City that Leeds won 1-0. However, 1978/79 brought Cherry seven goals, his most in a season. During a memorable campaign as Leeds qualified for Europe, Cherry grabbed a goal on the opening day of the season at Arsenal in a 2-2 draw, notched the winner in an exciting 3-2 win against Ipswich and opened the scoring in a 5-1 win at home to Bolton Wanderers.

Initially the only uncapped member of the first team; his consistent performances brought him international recognition. Winning 27 England caps, he is one of only two Leeds United players to captain his country (v. Australia in 1980), but never played in a team that qualified for a major tournament. Unfortunately, he also holds the distinction of being one of the few England players to be sent off in a full international, his dismissal coming in a bad-tempered encounter against Argentina in Buenos Aires in 1977. He was unlucky though, having had two teeth knocked out!

Player of the Year in 1980/81, his last experiences at Elland Road ended in heartache as Leeds suffered relegation to the Second Division after eighteen years in the top-flight, a far cry from when he joined in 1972. In the clear out that followed, Cherry joined Bradford City as player-manager before being promoted to manager. After guiding them to the Second Division, he experienced the downside of football management when he was dismissed in 1987. Tenth on the all-time appearances list at Leeds United, Trevor Cherry's football career will be recalled for his decade at Elland Road where he made 477 (+8 substitute) appearances, scoring 32 goals, and was immensely loyal.

ALLAN CLARKE

Allan Clarke was one of English football's most feared strikers during the late 1960s and early 1970s and entered Leeds United folklore when he scored the only goal of the 1972 FA Cup final. Nicknamed 'Sniffer' due to his instinctive goal-poaching ability, Clarke was top drawer and renowned as one of Europe's most clinical finishers; his chilling efficiency when one-on-one with a goalkeeper was extraordinary.

Born in Willenhall on 31 July 1946, Clarke was the most famous of five footballing brothers. He made his Walsall debut at sixteen before honing his skills alongside George Cohen and Johnny Haynes at Fulham. Clearly impressed, Leicester City paid a British-record £150,000 for his services in May 1968, and during a turbulent season Clarke won the Man of the Match award in the FA Cup final before moving to Elland Road for another British record fee, £165,000. Clarke would be the final piece of Don Revie's great side.

His debut for Leeds was in the club's Charity Shield win over Manchester City; a week later he scored on his league debut against Tottenham Hotspur. Linking up with Mick Jones in attack, they formed a formidable partnership, terrorising opposing defences wherever they played. Few bettered the Clarke-Jones partnership, and if that wasn't sufficient, 'Hotshot' Lorimer was supporting them!

At the end of the 1969/70 season, which saw Leeds nearly pulled off a unique treble, Clarke scored a penalty on his full England debut against Czechoslovakia during the World Cup finals in Mexico. Carrying on his superb form in 1970/71, he scored in the final of the Fairs Cup against Juventus, winning his first major honour as a player. In 1971/72, Leeds played breathtaking football, but for Clarke and Leeds supporters one memory stands out, his flying header in the Centenary FA Cup final against Arsenal, when he again won the Man of the Match award.

Clarke was at the peak of his career and, following the club's cup final disappointments in 1973, finally gained a League Championship medal in 1973/74 after finishing a runner-up

Clarke goes close against Manchester United (above), and scores against Swindon Town (opposite above) during Leeds' run to the 1970 FA Cup Final.

on three occasions. Although not his most prolific term as a goalscorer, he did score the winning goal in the penultimate game of the season; an incredibly tense affair at home to Ipswich Town that finished 3-2. The result ultimately clinched the title.

Following Don Revie's departure in the close season, one challenge remained for his former players, the European Cup. During a memorable campaign, Clarke scored a crucial goal against Barcelona in the semi-finals to help Leeds reach the final but tragically, Europe's premier trophy eluded them.

As Revie's legends moved on, Clarke teamed up with Joe Jordan and Duncan McKenzie. Although no longer title contenders, Leeds were unlucky not to win any silverware, falling at the semi-final stage of the FA Cup and League Cup. Following knee surgery in 1977, Clarke knew his playing days at the top level were ending, but not before notching his 150th Leeds goal against Middlesbrough in 1978.

An England regular in the early 1970s, Clarke scored 10 goals in 19 appearances, and struck in some memorable encounters including when England defeated Austria 7-0 and Scotland 5-0. He also scored during England's infamous World Cup exit to Poland in 1973 following a 1-1 draw.

In an era when defences offered few opportunities, Clarke's speed off the mark and instant touch gave him a split second to cause damage, but he was also adept at harrying opponents into errors. Clarke's finishing ability set him apart. An assassin, he could waltz around a goalkeeper with nonchalant ease, catch a defender for pace, or place a shot or header into the net with deadly accuracy. A marksman of the highest calibre, he would punish every mistake by a defender.

Prior to the start of the 1978/79 season, Clarke joined Barnsley as player-manager. After leading them to promotion, he returned to manage Leeds in September 1980. Supporters welcomed Clarke's return but in trying circumstances, his key signings such as Peter Barnes at £930,000 failed to produce the goods. During a traumatic campaign in 1981/82 Leeds lost their fight for survival on the last day of the season. Clarke went on to guide Scunthorpe United before returning for a second spell with Barnsley, experiencing promotion, relegation, and numerous giant-killing acts in cup competitions before retiring from the game.

Still a regular visitor to Elland Road, Clarke always receives a terrific reception. The club's Player of the Year in 1972/73, Sniffer was top-scorer for Leeds United on four occasions, is the club's third-highest goalscorer with 151 goals in 361 (+5 substitute) appearances, but the abiding memory is his historic header at Wembley in 1972.

DAVID COCHRANE

David Cochrane joined Leeds United in 1937. Blessed with wonderful ability, his promising career was cut short due to the Second World War.

Born in Portadown on 14 August 1920, outside right Cochrane was the son of a former Irish star and could frighten the best of defenders with his pace, ball control and dribbling skills. He played for his hometown club at fifteen and signed professional forms shortly after his sixteenth birthday.

During the 1936/37 season in Ireland, 14 goals in 13 starts attracted the attention of numerous clubs. Leeds manager Billy Hampson was so impressed he persuaded the board at Elland Road to pay £2,000 for the youngster's services. Cochrane was one of the best young talents in the First Division when he made his League debut against Derby County in 1938. The youngster notched his first goal for the club in his next match, Leeds' record-breaking 8-2 win against Lincoln City, and stayed in the side until the last match, against Sheffield United, before the outbreak of war.

Leeds United c.1950. David Cochrane seated extreme left.

DAVID COCHRANE

Cochrane was the second Leeds United player to represent Northern Ireland, and became one of the youngest players to represent his country when he made his full debut in 1938 against England at Old Trafford aged eighteen. He would have won more than the 12 caps that came his way, but the war years curtailed his international career. During the conflicts, apart from 13 appearances for Leeds, Cochrane returned home to play for Portadown, Shamrock Rovers and Linfield, where he won a cup winners medal in 1945.

When league football resumed, Cochrane returned to Elland Road along with a number of his former colleagues, but age had caught up with several key players and as the 1946/47 season developed, it told on their fitness. Leeds had their worst season ever, winning just six matches. Relegation came long before the final games.

Hampson was replaced by former Leeds legend Willis Edwards, but Edwards only managed to improve the players' fitness, not overall results during his spell in charge. Cochrane grabbed 7 goals in 1947/48, including a brace on the final day of the season as the team ended Edwards' tenure on a high with a 5-1 win against Bury.

Major Frank Buckley took the helm and Cochrane survived the clear out that followed and remained one of the most popular players with supporters. A regular in the first team, at the end of his last full campaign in 1949/50, Leeds finished fifth and reached the FA Cup quarter-finals for the first time in the club's history. Cochrane scored twice in a 3-0 win against Tottenham during a purple patch at the turn of the year that brought six successive wins and scored twice during the cup run.

Two games into the 1950/51 campaign Cochrane retired from playing after 185 appearances, scoring 32 goals. Though much of Cochrane's career was played in the Second Division, those fortunate to see him play recall his sublime skills and testify that he was one of the best wingers to represent Leeds United.

TOM COCHRANE

Tom Cochrane joined Leeds United shortly after the club's return to top-flight football as Second Division runners-up in 1927/28. It took this dangerous winger time to settle but he eventually demonstrated his prowess.

Born in Newcastle upon Tyne, on 7 October 1908, Cochrane tried to break through into the professional ranks, but failed despite having trials with a number of clubs. Fortunately, United manager Dick Ray saw him play while in charge of Doncaster Rovers and had been impressed, but was unable to make him an offer at the time.

Once Ray had assessed the depth of the Leeds squad prior to the start of the 1928/29 season, he decided to look at Cochrane again and duly offered the youngster his first professional contract. Despite a brilliant display on his debut against Manchester City, it took Cochrane time to break into the first team due to the form of left-winger Tom Mitchell.

Mitchell's popularity with supporters was a problem for Cochrane, because any error was spotted by the Elland Road faithful. It also didn't help Cochrane that the team was inconsistent, finishing fifth in 1929/30, their highest finish at the time in the First Division, only to suffer relegation the following term!

Gradually though, Cochrane overcome crowd taunts with his skilful wing play and by the start of the 1931/32 season had cemented his place in the first team. The players were determined to regain their top-flight status at the first attempt. Two wins in the last ten games cost the title, but the runners-up spot in 1931/32 was rarely in doubt.

The league campaign turned out to be a triumph for the club with Cochrane, who became one of the key players in the team's success that term, missing only one league game throughout the season. Tormenting defenders up and down the country, he linked brilliantly with Billy Furness and Charlie Keetley in attack to end the league campaign third top scorer with 9 goals; his best return during his eight-year spell at the club. Among his tally was the winning strike in a 3-2 victory over Millwall. Cochrane grabbed his only braces for Leeds in 5-0 wins against Oldham Athletic and Burnley.

Competing against the best defenders in the country, Leeds finished the next two league campaigns in the top ten, the highlight a club-record 8-0 win over Leicester City in 1934. However, the 1934/35 season would be anything but comfortable. Throughout a difficult campaign, Leeds struggled and towards the latter stages of the season Billy Hampson replaced Ray as manager. It was tight, but Leeds avoided relegation with a fine run in the last six matches.

Cochrane played one more term as a regular for Leeds before joining Middlesbrough and briefly Bradford Park Avenue, but it was during his career at Leeds United when he made 259 appearances, scoring 27 goals, that he excelled. Justifying the faith Ray had in him, Tom Cochrane, who died in 1976, was a classy and dangerous winger during the early 1930s.

Bobby Collins may have been small in stature but he was a giant on the pitch. Joining Leeds in March 1962 for £25,000 from Everton, thirty-one-year-old Collins was Don Revie's best signing and arguably the most important in the club's history.

Born in Glasgow on 16 February 1931, Revie knew Collins' calibre as he had made his name at Celtic in the 1950s where he won a League title, the Scottish Cup and Scottish League Cup. It was in this latter competition in 1958 that Collins was part of the team that destroyed Rangers 7-1 at Hampden Park, guaranteeing him a place in Celtic folklore.

BOBBY COLLINS

Collins, dubbed the Wee Barra by Celtic followers, endeared himself to players and supporters alike with his all-action game. A brilliant tactician and motivator, Collins was a superb passer of the ball and possessed a thunderous strike, bamboozling many a goalkeeper with his trademark 'banana' shot. Collins always made his presence known and never shirked a tackle. His reputation preceded him but there was little opponents could do. Playing with and against the stars of a golden era, Collins held his own against the elite.

During eight years at his hometown club Collins played alongside Bertie Auld, Charlie Tulley and Jock Stein and is one of a rare number of players to score a hat-trick of penalties in a match; his feat coming against Aberdeen in 1953. He represented the Scottish League on numerous occasions and won the first of 31 Scottish caps while at Parkhead. A star for the national team during the mid-1950s, he scored for his country in the 1958 World Cup finals in Sweden. After achieving everything in Scottish football, Collins joined Everton for £23,000 in September 1958, where he enhanced his reputation over four seasons.

When Collins arrived at Elland Road, Leeds sat bottom of the table. Unless there was a rapid improvement in the remaining eleven games, Revie's team would be playing in the Third Division for the first time in the club's history. Collins' impact was immediate. A goal on his debut against Swansea Town brought a welcome win, and following a number of gritty displays, safety was assured in the last game at Newcastle United after a 3-0 win.

Collins inspired the club's great escape with his never-say-die attitude. He also brought the best out of future stars such as Jack Charlton, Billy Bremner, Albert Johannesson and Willie Bell. It marked a major turning point in the club's history.

Revie blooded teenagers Gary Sprake, Paul Reaney and Norman Hunter as Leeds finished fifth in 1962/63. Collins grabbed a brace against Grimsby Town and scored in fine victories against Plymouth Argyle 6-1 and Swansea 5-0.

With the arrival of Johnny Giles and Alan Peacock the following term, and with Collins acting as the midfield anchor, Revie's mix of youth and experience blended perfectly as the Second Division title was secured. Bizarrely, in the six games in which Collins scored, Leeds won! In 1964/65, the double was tantalisingly close as Leeds amazed everyone by finishing runners-up in both the League and FA Cup. It was a remarkable campaign, when among many highlights Collins grabbed 10 goals, his highest return at Leeds, including a brace in comfortable wins against Blackpool and Burnley and the only goal of a classic league encounter at Manchester United.

Despite the disappointment, a golden era had dawned at Leeds. Collins became the first player in the club's history to lead a team out at Wembley and his efforts earned him the last of his Scottish caps, after an absence of five years, and he also picked up the prestigious Footballer of the Year award, the first Leeds player to do so.

The 1965/66 campaign, however, ended prematurely for Collins when in Leeds' first tilt at the Fairs Cup his thighbone was shattered following a horrendous challenge in Torino. Although he regained full fitness, Collins would play just seven more games for Leeds. Following brief spells at Bury and Morton, he embarked on a number of coaching positions before retiring from the game.

In the club's history few players have had as much impact as this amazing player. Scoring 26 goals in 167 appearances, Leeds United supporters will never forget Bobby Collins' endeavours that heralded a golden era for the club.

Terry Cooper began his playing career as an out-and-out winger before converting to a swashbuckling left-back on a regular basis at the start of the 1967/68 campaign. Within two years, Cooper was world class, his pace enabling him to support the attack with devastating effect.

Born in Brotherton, on 12 July 1944, Cooper joined Leeds' rich crop of youngsters as an apprentice in 1961 and made his debut during the 1963/64 Second Division campaign. His opening games were a baptism of fire. On his debut against Swansea City, Leeds clinched promotion; on his second appearance at Charlton Athletic, the team clinched the title!

On his occasional appearances during the next three years, Cooper got used to crucial matches as a replacement for left-winger Albert Johannesson or left-back Willie Bell. Memorable call-ups included FA Cup semi-final clashes against Manchester United and Chelsea, and both legs of the club's first European final against Dynamo Zagreb. He also notched his first goal for the club at Aston Villa in August 1965, a campaign when he scored four goals in all competitions, his best return in a season.

The 1967/68 campaign finally saw Cooper make his mark in the number three shirt. A keen tackler, tactically astute and possessing natural pace, Cooper developed a tremendous understanding with Eddie Gray on the left flank. His experience as a winger helped him in his role as an overlapping full-back who could set up chances for his strikers with pinpoint crosses, and he was also able to anticipate his opponents' thoughts when defending as a former winger. Playing Cooper alongside Paul Reaney, Jack Charlton and Norman Hunter meant Revie now had a balanced defence that would become the most reliable around.

In a memorable League Cup run, Cooper scored one goal, but what a crucial strike; the winner against Arsenal in the final at Wembley; the club's first 'major' honour. Within months, Leeds had claimed the Fairs Cup, following an aggregate win over Hungarian giants Ferencvaros. Cooper could not have timed his elevation to the first team better.

A key member of the First Division title-winning team in 1968/69, Cooper helped Leeds defeat Manchester City in the Charity Shield before playing his part in the club's 'treble' bid in 1969/70. For Cooper though there would be no rest after the FA Cup final defeat to Chelsea, because he was a regular for his country, having made his debut for England in a 5-0 win over France in March 1969.

Within days, he was flying off to the World Cup finals in Mexico, a tournament acknowledged as the greatest football spectacle ever. His performances in the competition, especially against Brazil in the qualifying section, would see him become recognised as the best left-back in the world. Some accolade!

Carrying on his superb form into the 1970/71 season, though Leeds lost out in the race for the First Division title to Arsenal, his displays against Juventus in the Fairs Cup final triumph enhanced his reputation as the best left-back around. With the football world seemingly at his feet, he broke a leg at Stoke City a week before Leeds' FA Cup semi-final win over Birmingham City in 1972. The injury sidelined him for nearly two years.

Although Cooper played a few more games for Leeds during the 1973/74 and 1974/75 campaigns, and made his twentieth and final appearance for England, he was unable to recapture his previous form. With Trevor Cherry in the side, Cooper's career at Leeds was over after fourteen seasons. Following spells at Middlesbrough and Bristol City, Cooper held

coaching and managerial posts at Bristol Rovers, Doncaster Rovers, Bristol City, Exeter City; guiding them to the Fourth Division title in 1989/90, and Birmingham City. Today, he works as a European scout for Southampton.

A wonderfully talented footballer, Terry Cooper made 340 (+11 substitute) appearances, scoring 11 goals for Leeds United, the most notable his terrific goal at Wembley in 1968. The finest left-back the club has produced; T.C. was simply world class.

Wilf Copping was one of the toughest centre-backs to play the game. However, although a ferocious tackler, he was not dubbed a dirty player for Leeds United, Arsenal or England during the 1930s.

Born in Barnsley on 17 August 1909, Dick Ray persuaded Copping to join Leeds from Middlecliffe Rovers in March 1929 but he did not make his debut until the start of the 1930/31 season. There was genuine belief that Leeds could challenge for the title after finishing the previous campaign fifth, their best performance since formation.

Copping made his debut against Portsmouth and remained an ever-present throughout what turned into a harrowing season. Occasionally Leeds were brilliant, as Blackpool and Middlesbrough experienced after conceding seven goals, but the majority of the campaign was a relegation battle, which was eventually lost on the last day of the season.

The players were determined to bounce back immediately; nine straight wins in the autumn confirming their desire. A poor run during the run-in cost Leeds the title, but the runners–up spot was rarely in doubt. Copping, Jack Milburn and Tom Cochrane were the only players to feature in at least forty games throughout the successful campaign. During the next two seasons, Leeds finished in the top ten, the highlight being the club's record-breaking 8-0 win over Leicester City in 1934.

Leeds United 1933/34. Back row: Hornby, George Milburn, Moore, Jones, Jack Milburn, Copping. Front row: Mahon, Roper, Hart, Keetley, Furness, Cochrane.

WILF COPPING

Playing against the best players in the country brought the best out of 'Iron Man' Copping. His distribution from defence was exceptional but his tackling ability became his trademark. Copping was a real character, and he could certainly intimidate an opponent. Before a game, he never shaved; his rugged appearance unnerving opponents before they even kicked a ball!

Copping's impressive displays were rewarded with two Football League representative appearances and international honours for England. After his debut against Italy in 1933, he went on to win seven caps while at Leeds. During this period, Copping formed a formidable partnership with Willis Edwards and Ernie Hart in Leeds defence. All three would play for England, but unfortunately never in the same game. One can only speculate what opposing international forwards would have made of this threesome!

Scoring in a 6-1 win against Newcastle United in 1932/33, one of only four goals by Copping for Leeds, it was only a matter of time before his status as one of the best stoppers in the game drew attention from high-profile clubs. At the end of the 1933/34 season Arsenal made an astonishing bid of £6,000 for his services, and the opportunity was too great for Leeds and Copping to turn down. At Highbury, Copping further enhanced his reputation, winning two First Division titles and the FA Cup. He also took his tally of England appearances to 20.

Copping returned to Leeds for a brief second spell in 1939 before the outbreak of the Second World War. During the hostilities, he played 28 wartime games for Leeds and 12 wartime representative matches before retiring. He trained the Army XI prior to taking up a number of coaching posts at the end of the war with Antwerp, Southend, Bristol City and the Belgium national team.

Leeds United followers have always warmed to a totally committed player who never shirks a tackle. Wilf Copping, who died in 1980, was such a player. A tremendous character; Copping's endeavours in 183 matches are now part of club folklore. His like would not be seen for three decades until Norman 'bites yer legs' Hunter arrived on the scene.

FRED CROOT

Fred Croot was one of the mainstays of the Leeds City team during their fifteen years in existence. Outside left Croot is one of only two players to make more than 200 appearances, with only legendary striker Billy McLeod playing more games and scoring more goals.

Born in Rushden in 1886, Croot played for Wellingborough and Sheffield United prior to his move to Yorkshire rivals Leeds City in 1907. Croot made his debut on the left wing in the opening fixture of the 1907/08 season at home to Glossop. City's 2-1 win was the first of three in the opening four fixtures. Gilbert Gillies' side also won their opening five fixtures at home but the remainder of the season would yield only four more victories on home soil as City slipped to twelfth spot.

Finishing second-top scorer with 8 goals behind McLeod, Croot was the only ever-present in the side and something of a lucky talisman when scoring. In the seven games Croot recorded a goal Leeds were unbeaten. Indeed, six of the games ended in victories, including a 5-2 win against Clapton Orient when Croot scored his first goal for the club and a brace in a 4-1 win against Grimsby.

The new campaign saw Frank Scott-Walford at the helm, but the new boss failed to improve City's league form. Croot was an integral part of the side and replaced McLeod as penalty taker in 1909/10, converting three spot kicks during the campaign. The following season Croot knocked in five and during 1911/12 scored two in a 4-3 win at Barnsley, City's last victory with Scott-Walford in charge. Croot's brace is also the only occasion a City player scored two penalties in a match.

Finishing second bottom of the table was the last straw for the City directors. Appointing Herbert Chapman manager, the new boss improved the forward line during 1912/13 and it brought immediate dividends. Scoring a club-record seventy goals, City finished sixth for the first time since their inaugural campaign. Croot scored 7 goals including three more penalties, taking his tally to 15, the most of any City player.

In 1913/14 City finished fourth, missing promotion by 2 points, but Croot would play only a cameo role, making 10 appearances due to the arrival of Ivan Sharpe, a member of the Great Britain side that won a gold medal at the 1912 Olympic Games. Following 5 appearances in 1914/15, when City finished fifteenth in the season before the First World War, Croot played 14 matches for Leeds during the hostilities before ending his career with a spell at Clydebank after the war.

Fred Croot was at Leeds City for all but two seasons of the club's tenure in the Football League. Scoring 38 goals in 227 matches, his name ranks alongside Billy McLeod and Herbert Chapman as one of the most influential characters in the early development of football in the City of Leeds.

H ilton Crowther is a name synonymous with the birth of Leeds United following the demise of Leeds City on 13 October 1919.

S. Whittham & Sons auctioned the players at the Metropole Hotel, Billy McLeod generating the greatest fee from Notts County of £1,250. Within hours, devastated supporters held a meeting at Salem Central Hall. Joe Henry jr was appointed chairman and adverts were placed in the local press for players. The new Leeds United joined the Midland League, replacing Leeds City reserves and then moved back into Elland Road after Yorkshire Amateurs agreed to leave.

The key to eventual success however was the financial support and dedication given by Crowther, then chairman of Huddersfield Town. Disillusioned with local support for his own club, rugby league being the main sport in the city, Crowther proposed to move Huddersfield 'lock stock and barrel' to Elland Road. Many of the players and Leeds United's board agreed. A new name, Leeds Trinity, was even discussed.

The Football League received Crowther's proposal and gave Huddersfield until 31 December 1919 to pay Crowther off, and in a further twist, Huddersfield supporters, shocked at the thought of losing their team, demanded a right to buy Crowther's £25,000 stake. Hilton Crowther meanwhile was by now the new chairman at Leeds, loaning £35,000 to be

January 1939. Leeds United's first chairman, Mr Hilton Crowther, is seated in the centre.

Leeds United 1923/24. From left to right, back row: Murrell (trainer), Bell, Coates, Robson, Armand, Menzies, Flood, Gordon, Noble, Duffield, Ure (assistant trainer). Third row: L. Baker, Frew, Smith, Hart, Morris, Bell, Swan, A. Baker, Gascoigne, Harris. Second row: Whalley, Johnson, Shirwin, Poyntz, Norman (team manager), Crowther, (chairman), Fairclough (secretary-manager), Richmond, Powell. Front row: Fullam, Down, Lambert, Mason, J. Baker (captain), Allen, Whipp, Speak.

repaid when First Division status had been achieved. He immediately began developing the club he was convinced had more long-term potential. Appointing Arthur Fairclough as team manager was an inspired decision.

Fairclough and his assistant Dick Ray brought in new players and as they found their footballing feet, Crowther travelled the country canvassing for votes to gain election to the Football League. With financial stability and the nucleus of a capable side assured, Crowther knew he had a good case. On 31 May 1920 his efforts were rewarded when Leeds polled the highest number of votes, thirty-one, to gain Football League status.

Although Leeds United lost their Division Two opening fixture to Port Vale, ironically the team that had replaced Leeds City, a new era had dawned. The newly formed club ended their inaugural season in the Football League in fourteenth place and with an average attendance of 16,000 the future looked promising for the club.

By the 1923/24 campaign the first team was ready to challenge for promotion. Within twelve months, Crowther's dream of First Division status had been achieved. At the end of the season, Crowther resigned as chairman, though he remained on the board until his death in 1957.

J. Hilton Crowther's investment of time and money must never be forgotten because without his efforts and inspired leadership the likes of John Charles, Don Revie, Billy Bremner and Gordon Strachan would never have been. Crowther is a giant of a man in the Leeds United story.

TONY CURRIE

Tony Currie was a born entertainer on a football pitch and Leeds United fans loved his unique abilities, following his £240,000 transfer in 1976. Playing in an era alongside the likes of Stan Bowles, Frank Worthington and Rodney Marsh, fans lapped up the exquisite skills on parade, however outrageous they appeared.

Born in London on 1 January 1950, after Chelsea rejected the talented teenager Watford signed Currie as a professional in 1967, where he won England Youth honours. Following 17 appearances, his budding reputation tempted Sheffield United to snap him up for £35,000.

At the Blades, Currie enhanced his skills. Possessing first-class ball control, his accurate passing and ability to score spectacular goals made him a star. His potential brought England Under-23 caps and a full England debut in 1972. His best year for the Blades came in 1974/75. Finishing sixth, their highest position for years, Currie's form was irresistible. One strike in particular against West Ham in front of the BBC's *Match of the Day* cameras when he beat one bewildered opponent four times before slotting the ball home brought rave reviews. Sheffield United's key player for a number of seasons, Currie became Jimmy Armfield's first purchase at Leeds.

Armfield knew central midfield players had to stamp their personality on a game and Currie fitted the bill. Seen as the ideal replacement for Johnny Giles, Currie was an instant hit with Leeds fans following his debut against West Brom on the opening day of the season. Flamboyant and blessed with unbelievable skill, his passing, shooting and vision were of the highest calibre. When running at opponents, his strength and touch on the ball was sensational, and after scoring Currie blew kisses to the crowd. Supporters loved it. Although he preferred to spray passes around the pitch, he could also battle for possession. Currie was just about the best around in the late 1970s.

Leeds ended the 1976/77 season comfortably mid-table; however, the season was best remembered for an FA Cup run, which saw the team reach the semi-finals. The following campaign, with Arthur Graham, Brian Flynn and Ray Hankin now at the club, there was further semi-final heartache, this time in the League Cup. Currie was the star player and his performances earned the club's Player of the Year award and a recall to the England team. Gaining a further 11 caps, taking his tally to 17, Currie struck glorious long-range goals against Wales and Hungary.

In 1978/79, with Jimmy Adamson at the helm, Leeds once again reached the semi-final of the League Cup. Alas, the tie against Southampton proved particularly traumatic as Leeds, 2-0 ahead in the opening leg at Elland Road, eventually lost 3-2 on aggregate. In the League,

Leeds' consistency brought European qualification but, after 124 appearances, Currie returned south, joining QPR in a £400,000 deal.

Currie went on to captain his new club in the 1982 FA Cup final, but persistent injuries prevented his career reaching similar heights again during brief spells at a number of non-league clubs. Still involved in the game, he has been a community officer at Sheffield United for more than a decade.

Whenever Tony Currie returns to Leeds, he always receives a warm reception from supporters who remember his elegant skills, panache and inventiveness. Always looking for the spectacular, Currie had an eye for a goal, and arguably his best strike was a superb twenty-five-yard 'banana' shot against Southampton in 1978. That moment for many supporters encapsulated this terrific player.

Mervyn Day was a tremendous servant to Leeds United during a period when supporters began to believe the team could become a force again. His performances, especially during the 1989/90 campaign, were particularly memorable as top-flight football returned to Elland Road.

Born in Chelmsford, 26 June 1955, Day's goalkeeping career at West Ham United got off to a superb start when he was part of the Hammers side that won the FA Cup in 1975 while still in his teens. Named PFA Young Player of the Year his form was so consistent he was tipped as a future England 'keeper after his performances for England's Youth and Under-23 teams. Unfortunately, a loss of form resulted in him losing his place to the more experienced Phil Parkes.

With limited prospects of first-team football, Day joined Leyton Orient at the end of the 1978/79 season before moving on to Aston Villa in 1983. After two years as a back-up 'keeper, he was in demand again when Eddie Gray brought him to Leeds United for £30,000. Gray pitched Day in immediately at Oldham Athletic, dispite Leeds winning their previous encounter 5-0 against Notts County. Rediscovering his form and confidence, Day's arrival at Leeds proved a turning point in his career.

After Billy Bremner took the helm at the club Day became a key figure in a revamped side, especially in 1986/87 when Leeds sensationally reached an FA Cup semi-final and so nearly

MERVYN DAY

Leeds United 1985/86 pre season photograph. Day is standing in the middle row, fourth from left.

won promotion back to the First Division. Agonisingly, Coventry won a classic semi-final and Charlton Athletic scored two late goals in the Second Division play-off final to win a dramatic encounter.

Following Howard Wilkinson's arrival a few games into the 1988/89 campaign, Day was one of the few players to stay in the side when Wilkinson's reshaped team kicked off the 1989/90 season as promotion favourites. Throughout a memorable campaign that culminated in Leeds clinching the Division Two championship, Day passed his 600th league appearance as a player. Brave, agile and reliable, Day was a model of consistency and his form was a major factor to the team's title success.

Among a number of notable saves during the season, arguably Day's most crucial came against Leicester City in the penultimate game of the campaign. With the scores locked at 1-1 and the tension unbearable inside the ground, Day stopped a scorching drive from future teammate Gary McAllister, before Gordon Strachan struck home a priceless winner near the end.

With promotion to the top-flight secure, John Lukic's arrival meant that Day had to settle for a role as cover. After 268 appearances, during the 1992/93 season, Day became player-coach but at the end of the campaign decided to join Carlisle United as player-coach. After helping Carlisle win the Third Division title in 1994/95, a season when they also reached the Auto Windscreens final, Day took over as manager for a spell, before moving back to London as a coach with Charlton Athletic.

Regarded as the best goalkeeper in the division during Leeds promotion campaign in 1989/90, Mervyn Day was a central figure in the rebirth of Leeds United as they began the road back to the top of English football.

TONY DORIGO

Tony Dorigo joined Leeds United during the summer of 1991 for £1.3m, having built a reputation as being one of the most stylish defenders around. Many observers believed the Australian was the best left-back in the country. Dorigo would demonstrate his skills on many occasions.

Born in Melbourne on 14 March 1963, Dorigo began his apprenticeship at Aston Villa in 1981 and made the most of his opportunity, winning 11 Under-21 caps for England. His potential was obvious and Chelsea paid £475,000 for his services in 1987. His first season saw the Blues relegated but the demotion gave the Londoners the opportunity to rebuild and the strategy was a success as Chelsea raced to the 1988/89 Second Division title; finishing 17 points clear of their nearest rivals.

Howard Wilkinson, having taken over the reigns at Elland Road, saw at first hand the capabilities of this exciting left-back as Leeds finished 32 points adrift! Playing in the First Division enhanced Dorigo's career as he won 6 full caps for his adopted country and scored the only goal of the 1990 Zenith Data Systems final at Wembley.

Dorigo's arrival at Elland Road was a tremendous coup for Wilkinson because the left-back position had been his biggest headache. Three previous occupiers, Glyn Snodin, Jim Beglin and Peter Haddock, had sustained long-term injuries; the latter two career-ending ones. Dorigo would be more fortunate.

Missing only four games during the 1991/92 campaign, following an opening day win against Nottingham Forest, Dorigo was a revelation, linking brilliantly with Gary Speed. Mixing his defensive role with raids down the left flank, Dorigo continuously supplied opportunities with pinpoint crosses for strikers Lee Chapman, Rod Wallace and Carl Shutt.

An intelligent player, Dorigo was always comfortable on the ball. Timing tackles to perfection, Dorigo anticipated danger and used his electric pace to make last-ditch tackles. Adept at changing the direction of play he also had an eye for a spectacular goal, as his majestic strikes against Manchester City, Norwich City and Sheffield Wednesday demonstrated. Dorigo's debut season was richly rewarded with a Championship medal as Leeds secured the First Division title and supporters voted him Player of the Year.

Dorigo began the 1992/93 campaign with a fortuitous goal in Leeds' 4-3 victory over Liverpool in the Charity Shield, and for three seasons was a key player at Elland Road. Taking his appearances for England to 15, he picked up a niggling injury during the 1995/96 campaign, which cost him a place in the League Cup final at Wembley. Although he returned

Tony Dorigo celebrates after scoring his first goal for Leeds United.

the following term, his days at Elland Road were over after 203 (+4 substitute) appearances and six years' excellent service. Dorigo went on play briefly for Torino, Derby County and Stoke City.

Leeds United supporters will remember Tony Dorigo for his swashbuckling displays during the 1991/92 Championship season. The best left-back at Leeds since the days of Terry Cooper, this likeable Aussie served the club with distinction.

ALBERT DUFFIELD ——————————————

Albert Duffield was one of Leeds United's most dependable performers following his arrival at the club in July 1920. A rock of the defence during the club's formative years, Duffield's endeavour was essential during what was an exciting yet uncertain period in Leeds United's history.

Born in Owston Ferry, Lincolnshire on 3 March 1894, 'Bert' Duffield began his football career with Gainsborough Trinity but after two seasons, his progress was halted following the outbreak of the First World War. Serving as a bombardier in France he returned home wounded, and after recovering from his injuries joined Midland League side Castleford Town.

Duffield's spell at Town was eventful. Impressive at right-back, he once agreed to play as an emergency striker and scored four goals! In the same league were Leeds United, and club officials were clearly impressed because when they gained entry to the Football League in May 1920, manager Arthur Fairclough persuaded twenty-six-year-old Duffield to join him at Elland Road.

Duffield made his Leeds debut against Port Vale in the club's first match in the Football League. During this historic season, he was one of three players, along with 'keeper Billy Down and skipper Jim Baker, to be ever-present in the side. The first three League campaigns would see gradual improvement and by 1923/24, the players were ready to push for promotion to the First Division. The campaign was underpinned by two winning streaks and they eventually wrapped up the title in the penultimate game of the season with a 1-0 win at home to Nelson.

Stepping up in class, life in the First Division was tough as the team battled for survival and Duffield eventually lost his place to Jimmy Allan after six games of the 1925/26 season.

ALBERT DUFFIELD

Leeds United 1920/21. From left to right, back row: Barker, Crowther (chairman), Duffield, Cooper, Hart, Brown, Jacklin, Downs, Cooper, Walton, Jeffries, Stead (assistant manager), Fairclough (manager), Murrell (trainer). Middle row: Frew, Spencer, Lyons, Elson, Thompson, Stuart, Goldthorpe, Reynolds. Front row: Armitage, Mason, Baker (captain), Tillotson, Musgrove, McGee, Best.

Following 211 appearances for Leeds, Duffield joined Bradford, who he served for three seasons before retiring from the game. Prior to his death in 1981, Duffield ran a poultry farm near Goole and coached a local football team in his spare time.

A strong, determined and reliable defender, Duffield rarely won headlines but never let his colleagues down throughout his years as a first-team player, especially co-defenders Baker, Jimmy Frew, Bill Menzies and young Ernie Hart. His consistency was quite extraordinary and his place in the side was never in doubt. Missing only thirteen matches during the club's opening five Football League campaigns, Duffield played his part as Leeds gained top-flight status for the first time.

Harry Duggan signed for Leeds United in May 1925. A hard-working inside right and occasional striker, Duggan created openings for colleagues with his enthusiasm and opportunism throughout much of the 1930s.

Born in Dublin on 8 June 1903, Duggan gained a reputation in junior football with Richmond United when he scored 49 goals in 1924/25. Snapped up by Arthur Fairclough, Duggan had to wait until September 1926 to make his debut in a home victory against Aston Villa. After a brief run in the side, Duggan was dropped as Leeds were relegated to the Second Division.

Dick Ray was appointed manager but Duggan would not play in the first team until the 1929/30 season when Leeds finished fifth in the First Division. Though not a Leeds regular, he was the club's first player to represent Northern Ireland (*v*. England, 1929). Already the first Leeds player to represent the Republic of Ireland (*v.* Italy B, 1927), Duggan now had the unusual distinction of being capped by two countries. He went on to win 8 caps for Northern Ireland and 5 for the Republic.

Duggan began the 1930/31 campaign by scoring 5 goals in 11 appearances, including a brace in a 7-0 win against Middlesbrough. The win, though, was a false dawn. Duggan played one match as Leeds suffered a terrible run of form, which ended in relegation. The players were determined to regain top-flight status in 1931/32 and this time Duggan was part of Ray's team. Playing 35 matches, he helped Leeds bounce back behind Champions Wolves, notching five goals, including the opening strike in a 5-2 win against Manchester United.

The following term Duggan helped Leeds record a rare double against Liverpool, the first of three in the club's history. Scoring in Leeds' 1-0 win at Anfield, Duggan scored the last goal in Leeds' 5-0 win at Elland Road. Liverpool may not have been the force they would become, but it is a remarkable fact that Duggan is the only Leeds player to score both home and away during a league campaign against the Reds, a feat he repeated in 1933/34 when Leeds lost 4-3 at Anfield before gaining revenge in the return with a thumping 5-1 victory!

Leeds finished in the top ten for a second consecutive season with Duggan playing as an emergency centre forward, Arthur Hydes being out through injury. Finishing with 11 goals to his credit, Duggan was second-top scorer behind Hydes, the highlight a club-record 8-0 win over Leicester City in April 1934 when Duggan scored a brace.

Although he scored a further 10 in 1934/35, including two goals in a 3-3 draw with Preston, the season was anything but comfortable. Billy Hampson replaced Ray during the campaign and Leeds only avoided relegation in the last six matches. In October 1936 Duggan joined Newport County, leading them to the Third Division (South) title in 1938/39.

Retiring the following season at the outbreak of the Second World War, Duggan served as an ARP warden before working for a glass company in Leeds prior to his death in 1968. Scoring 49 goals in 196 appearances, Harry Duggan was a diligent player for Leeds United, displaying a commendable attitude during nine years at the club.

Jimmy Dunn was one of the club's most consistent performers throughout the 1950s as top-flight football came back to Elland Road. Indeed, between 1952/53 and 1956/57 he only missed only one out of 217 league and cup games!

Born in Rutherglen on 23 October 1922, Dunn was a fine Scottish prospect at right-back while playing for junior side Rutherglen Glencairn. He served as a Royal Marine during the Second World War and looked like signing for Arbroath until Leeds manager Willis Edwards stepped in to sign him during the 1947/48 close season.

Following his debut in November 1947 at Cardiff City, Dunn struggled alongside his teammates throughout a difficult campaign, and it came as no surprise that when new boss Major Frank Buckley took over, he immediately rang the changes the following term.

In his new-look team, Dunn settled in alongside the likes of Eric Kerfoot, John Charles and Tommy Burnden. Gradually results improved and Leeds reached the quarter-finals of the FA Cup for the first time in 1949/50. The run ended at eventual cup-winners Arsenal. Leeds finished the league campaign in fifth place, with Dunn scoring what would be his only goal for the club during a 2-1 win against Blackburn Rovers in the penultimate match of the season.

Leeds United 1957. Jimmy Dunn is second from left on the back row.

Five more top-ten finishes followed in as many years. By 1955/56 Raich Carter was manager and with Leeds missing out on promotion the previous season by just 1 point, fans believed Leeds were in with a chance this time. Unfortunately, the team started slowly until Carter switched Charles to centre forward and gave Jack Charlton his first extended run in the team at centre half.

Although Charles began scoring, the team was a long way off the pace. However, Leeds won eight of their remaining nine games to snatch the runners-up spot behind Sheffield Wednesday. It had been mighty close and but for a 4-1 victory at Hull City in the last game Leeds would have missed out for a second successive season.

Nine years after being relegated Leeds had won promotion and Dunn, the only player in the side to have been at the club throughout this period, could now test himself against the likes of Stanley Matthews, Len Shackleton, Duncan Edwards and Nat Lofthouse. An ever-present throughout the promotion and Division One campaign, along with Roy Wood and Eric Kerfoot, Dunn remained in the first team during 1957/58 before spending much of his last season at Leeds as a squad member.

Dunn's consistency was quite extraordinary. He and left-back Grenville Hair occupied the numbers two and three shirts for eight seasons, missing only 45 games between them in 349 league and cup matches, and 32 of those came in two campaigns!

After a brief spell at Darlington, a knee injury forced Dunn to retire from the game. Consistently overlooked by Scottish selectors, he was unlucky not to win a full cap for his country. A regular at Leeds games for many years, prior to retiring Dunn assisted at Scarborough and worked for the Post Office.

Jimmy Dunn made 443 appearances for Leeds United during an eleven-year association with the club. Although it took a number of years to develop a side capable of challenging for promotion, players of Dunn's calibre and loyalty played their part and were essential to eventual success.

WILLIS EDWARDS

Willis Edwards enjoyed a thirty-eight-year association with Leeds United, serving as a player, coach, scout and manager. During fourteen seasons as a player Edwards was a class act. It would not have been difficult for him to join a more fashionable team like some of his colleagues, but his loyalty to the club was absolute, so he chose to battle away as Leeds found their feet in the Football League.

Born in Newport, near Alfreton, on 28 April 1905, Edwards' career began at Chesterfield, where he made his debut in 1919 aged seventeen. During his time at the club, Edwards was part of a revolution in the game as the Football League expanded to four divisions in 1921/22. Making his league debut in the Third Division (North), Edwards' displays won him acclaim as a player of potential.

Edwards realised that to progress he needed to be playing top-flight football. His opportunity came in 1924/25 when he joined Leeds United, struggling in their inaugural campaign in the First Division, for £1,500. Brought in to help shore up the defence, whether Edwards' signing proved the decisive factor in the club's survival that term is debatable, but his arrival coincided with an immediate improvement in results. After a winning debut against Liverpool in March 1925; only the club's eighth win that term, Leeds went on to finish just above the relegation zone.

Playing in the First Division brought the best out of Edwards. His passing ability, ball control, distribution and incisive tackling gained him a tremendous reputation and England's selectors recognised his outstanding performances in a trial match at Newcastle. Within weeks, he made his international debut against Wales. The first Leeds player to represent England, he also has the distinction of being the 500th player to play for his country.

By 1929, Edwards was the best wing half around and his 12th cap brought him the ultimate honour when he captained his country (v. Ireland), the first Leeds United player to do so. In his next international against Wales, club history was made when Edwards lined up alongside Ernie Hart; the first time two Leeds players had represented England together.

Skipper on his last five appearances, taking his tally of caps to 16, Edwards was indispensable throughout the 1920s despite Leeds' poor domestic form. Indeed, following relegation to the Second Division in 1926/27, Edwards' place in the England side was never in doubt, even though he was the only player playing outside the top division. In addition to England honours, Edwards also played for the Football League on 11 occasions, another club record.

Edwards made 444 appearances for Leeds, scoring 6 goals. Apart from two seasons, Edwards played all his football for Leeds in the First Division. Not that the team stayed in the Second Division long – on both occasions Edwards' drive and determination was a key factor in the renaissance that followed. Leeds won promotion at the first attempt in both 1927/28 and 1931/32.

Willis Edwards as
manager in 1947.

During Edwards' era, Leeds achieved four top-ten finishes and their fifth place in 1929/30, the best since formation, was not be bettered for thirty-five years. In addition there were two record victories, which still stand. Edwards played his part in both games when first Crystal Palace were slaughtered 8-1 in an FA Cup tie in 1930 and four years later he returned from a spell out through injury to help his team demolish Leicester City 8-0 in a First Division clash.

His latter years would see Leeds mainly struggle; surviving two relegation battles in 1934/35 and 1936/37, but while at the club Edwards played with some fine players. One partnership stood out: the half-back line of Edwards-Hart-Copping. Unfortunately, although Edwards and Hart played in victories over Ireland and Wales, the three England careers never crossed, so one can only speculate how opposing forwards would have coped when lining up against them!

The war years cut short his outstanding career, although he did play 24 wartime games for Leeds, scoring twice. When League football resumed in 1946/47 he soon found a role within the club he had served so proudly. Initially he helped trainer Bob Roxborough look after the reserves, but as relegation loomed for the first team, he replaced manager Billy Hampson.

Edwards began the difficult task of rebuilding the team, and certainly improved their fitness levels, but after a year he returned to his coaching position, before serving as a scout during the 1950s. Willis Edwards died in 1988. One of the all-time greats at Leeds United, his endeavours on behalf of the club were outstanding.

———————————————— ARTHUR FAIRCLOUGH

Arthur Fairclough was appointed Leeds United manager on 26 February 1920 and holds the honour of guiding the newly formed club to their first success as Second Division Champions in 1923/24.

Born in Redbrook near Barnsley in March 1873, poor health blighted his playing career but he became Barnsley's secretary when they joined the Football League in 1898. After three years, he left due to business commitments but returned to the game after election to the Sheffield Football Association in 1902. A qualified referee, he returned to Barnsley as secretary-manager in 1904; guiding his hometown team to an FA Cup triumph over West Bromwich Albion in 1912, a result which made up for their cup final defeat against Newcastle United in 1910.

Following Barnsley's cup triumph, Huddersfield Town chairman J. Hilton Crowther, appointed Fairclough secretary-manager, and during his tenure helped lay the foundations for the successes that would follow under former Leeds City manager Herbert Chapman.

When Crowther took the helm as Leeds United's chairman, Fairclough was soon manager at Leeds, succeeding ex-Leeds City player Dick Ray, who became his assistant. While competing in the Midland League, the new management team searched for new players as Crowther travelled the country canvassing for votes to gain election to the Football League. Elected to the Second Division in May 1920, Fairclough appointed Jim Baker club captain and although Leeds lost their first game to Port Vale, the team improved gradually over three seasons.

Dick Norman replaced Ray as Fairclough's assistant in June 1923, which was the prelude to an historic campaign. Considered candidates for promotion in 1923/24, Fairclough's optimism was rewarded when top-flight football was assured for the first time. The promotion campaign was underpinned by two winning streaks, but the title was not clinched until a 1-0 victory against Nelson at Elland Road in the penultimate game of the season.

Unfortunately, during the club's initial First Division spell the team struggled, finishing in the bottom four each season, and but for a 4-1 win on the last day of the 1925/26 season when Tom Jennings grabbed a brace, would have been relegated. The following term the inevitable did happen, despite Jennings' tremendous haul of 35 goals in 41 games. Fairclough resigned and returned briefly to manage Barnsley in 1929 before retiring from the game.

It is eighty-five years since Arthur Fairclough, who died in 1948, became Leeds United's manager. The club was decades away from being a major force in the game when he was at the helm, but it is noteworthy that players such as Baker, Jennings, Willis Edwards, Ernie Hart and Bill Menzies, all of whom Fairclough brought to Elland Road during the formative years, are acknowledged as legends at the club. Their manager justifiably holds the same status.

CHRIS FAIRCLOUGH

Chris Fairclough was one of Howard Wilkinson's first signings for Leeds United in March 1989. An elegant footballer, Fairclough rarely made a costly error and was the central figure in defence during the club's title triumphs of the early 1990s.

Born in Nottingham on 12 April 1964, Fairclough began his career as an apprentice at Nottingham Forest in 1981, winning the first of 7 England Under-21 caps before moving to Tottenham Hotspur for £387,000 in 1987. Joining Leeds, initially on loan, Fairclough made his debut against Portsmouth and helped his new club consolidate their position in the Second Division before completing a £500,000 transfer during the 1988/89 close season.

A stalwart of the side that won the Second Division title on the last day of the 1989/90 season, Fairclough had natural pace, was composed during crucial phases of a game and chipped in with eight goals; including a crucial header at Oxford United as Leeds overhauled a two-goal deficit to win 4-2. Fairclough won the club's Player of the Year award at the end of his first full season.

The team surprised many pundits during their first campaign back in top-flight football, for eight seasons, by finishing fourth. As for Fairclough, who scored the first goal in an opening day 3-2 win at Everton, teaming up with Chris Whyte, he adapted to life in the First Division as if he had never been away. Nobody though could have predicted the events of the 1991/92 season as Leeds won a titanic battle over Manchester United to clinch the First Division championship.

Leeds show off the First Division trophy in front of the Kop, 2 May 1992. From left to right, back row: Chapman, Dorigo, Whyte, McClelland, Lukic, Cantona, Sterland, Batty, McAllister. Front row: Newsome, Hodge, Fairclough, Strachan, Wallace, Speed.

Chris Fairclough opens his scoring account for the 1991/92 season with this strike against Crystal Palace.

Wilkinson was astute in partnering Fairclough with Chris Whyte. Gelling from the start, the duo were one of the key factors in the club's ultimate championship success. There were many displays of note, but during the final five games when the pressure was at its most intense the Fairclough-Whyte partnership was immense. Four ended in victories, with just two goals conceded, and Fairclough scored his most crucial goal for Leeds when he broke the deadlock against Coventry City in the third of these games.

A member of the team that won the Charity Shield at Wembley against Liverpool, injury restricted his appearances in the inaugural Premier League season. In 1993/94 Fairclough was back to his best, missing just two league games as Leeds finished fifth. However, a long-term injury meant he would start just one league game the following term. Strong, courageous, a firm tackler and tactically astute, Fairclough served Leeds with distinction; making 232 (+9 substitute) appearances in his six seasons at the club, but it was time for a new challenge.

Joining Bolton Wanderers for £1m in July 1995, within two seasons Fairclough helped Bolton win the Division One title in 1996/97. An ever-present during their promotion campaign, after three seasons he joined Notts County, but after a brief spell ended his playing days at York City, retiring from the game in 2001. Currently completing a UEFA coaching badge, Chris Fairclough enjoyed a fine career at Leeds United during their return to the top.

Brian Flynn was a pocket-sized midfield dynamo for Leeds United during a transitional phase in the club's history. One of the shortest footballers to represent the club at just 5ft 3in, Flynn was among the most respected players of his era.

Born in Port Talbot on 12 October 1955, Flynn began his career at Burnley under the tutelage of Jimmy Adamson; making his debut in October 1972, but had no hesitation in joining Leeds for £175,000 when Jimmy Armfield offered him the opportunity in November 1977. A seasoned international for Wales, Flynn arrived at Leeds with an impressive track record and appeared a fine addition to Armfield's squad as Don Revie's stars moved on. After making his debut against Norwich City, within a year his former Burnley boss was at the helm at Elland Road.

It was difficult following previous stalwarts, but Flynn handled the pressure well and became a key member of the team. Forming a terrific partnership with Tony Currie in midfield, Flynn's work rate and tenacity combined with Currie's skill on the ball and flamboyance was a wonderful balance. Supported by Arthur Graham and Carl Harris down the flanks, Leeds produced exciting football.

A hustler, Flynn buzzed around midfield harrying opponents into errors. He also chipped in with the odd goal, his most memorable proving to be the winner at Manchester United in 1981, the last time a Leeds team won at Old Trafford. On the international scene, he continued to play regularly for Wales, his 32 appearances while at Leeds taking his total to 66, making him one of his country's most capped midfield players.

Although he failed to win any silverware with Leeds, he came close, playing in two League Cup semi-finals. During his first four seasons at Elland Road, Leeds finished in the top half of the table, qualifying for Europe in 1978/79, a season when Flynn was voted Player of the Year, but sadly, his fifth term brought relegation. In the clear out that followed, Flynn was one of the first players to depart after playing just two games in the Second Division.

Initially he joined former club Burnley, prior to brief spells at Cardiff City, Doncaster Rovers, Bury and Wrexham. Back in his homeland, Flynn experienced mixed fortunes as a player, caretaker-manager and player-manager before finally retiring in 1993 after twenty-one seasons as a professional footballer.

As a manager, Flynn rebuilt Wrexham after they finished bottom of the Football League in 1990/91. Within three seasons, he had guided them to promotion, and during his tenure presided over a number of giant-killing acts, the most notable in the FA Cup against Arsenal in 1992. After more than a decade at the helm he departed in 2001 but continues to work in the game.

Brian Flynn's finest years as a player were at Leeds United, where he made 174 (+3 substitute) appearances. In the middle of the park when the battle for possession was at its most intense, few opponents got the better of him.

BILLY FURNESS

Billy Furness was playing non-league football for Usworth Colliery when Dick Ray offered him the opportunity to join Leeds United in August 1928 for a transfer fee of £50. Furness would become one of the club's most dangerous strikers and his consistency made him invaluable during the post-war years at Elland Road.

Born in County Durham on 8 June 1909, Furness, made his debut in a home clash against Middlesbrough during the 1929/30 season; a campaign when Leeds finished fifth, their highest placing at that time. Furness, however, had to wait until the following term to class himself as regular but it must have been some experience.

In the third game of the season, Furness opened his account for Leeds during a 3-1 defeat at Arsenal before scoring his first goal at Elland Road a week later in a 4-2 win against Blackburn Rovers. On their day, Leeds could be brilliant, as thumping wins over Blackpool 7-3 and Manchester United 5-0 would suggest. Furness scored in both games but these results belied spells of inconsistency. The campaign was a long battle against relegation, which was lost on the last day of the season.

In 1931/32 promotion was rarely in doubt following nine consecutive wins during the autumn. Leeds should have won the title, but a poor run near the end of the season ended that hope. However, the runners-up spot was adequate compensation. With Furness playing alongside Charlie Keetley and Joe Firth, Leeds plundered plenty of goals. Furness grabbed a dozen, including eight in consecutive games in the first half of the campaign.

The following term proved to be a personal triumph for Furness, because not only did Leeds finish eighth but his consistency at inside left resulted in a call-up to the England squad at the end of the season. After playing against Italy, he went on the post-season tour of Hungary and Czechoslovakia.

The 1933/34 campaign brought another top-ten finish, but would be best remembered for a league clash in April 1934 when Leeds recorded a club-record 8-0 win over Leicester City, Furness scoring twice. Thereafter, in the main Leeds struggled at the wrong end of the table. Billy Hampson replaced Ray as manager during the latter stages of the 1934/35 season as the team flirted with relegation.

Leeds eventually survived following a late run when they lost just one of their last six matches. The hero was Furness, who scored seven goals in five games, including both goals in a 2-1 win at Derby County and a brace in Leeds 4-3 win against Tottenham Hotspur in the final game of the season. His 16 goals during the campaign was his best return while at Leeds.

Two seasons later the team was involved in another relegation battle. Furness was by now in and out of the side, but got a recall for the final two league games, which Leeds had to win to secure their position as a top-flight club. Furness rose to the challenge, scoring in victories over Sunderland and Portsmouth. These games would be his last for Leeds and were a fitting finale.

During the close season, Furness joined Norwich City for £2,700. After the Second World War, he played for a short period before taking up a position as trainer-coach. Billy Furness, who died in 1980, was a great supporting striker during the 1930s for Leeds United, scoring 66 goals and creating countless chances for his colleagues in 257 games for the club.

Johnny Giles was a central figure in Don Revie's legendary Leeds side for more than a decade following his arrival at Elland Road in August 1963. One of the great midfield generals of his era, Giles possessed exceptional passing ability, was a master tactician, scored his share of goals and could mix it with the best.

Born in Dublin on 6 January 1940, Giles developed at a number of local clubs, including Home Farm, before moving to England in 1957 to serve his apprenticeship at Manchester United. An FA Cup winner in 1963, when Giles failed to agree terms with Matt Busby during the close season he dropped down a division to join Revie at Leeds for £33,000. His signing would be one of the finest in the club's history.

Initially an outside right for Leeds, Giles arrived at Leeds feeling he had something to prove and played his part throughout the race for promotion in 1963/64. Missing only two games, after a winning debut against Bury, his goal at Swansea helped secure top-flight football, the title confirmed in the last game at Charlton. Buoyed with confidence the team astonished everyone in 1964/65 by finishing runners-up in both the League and FA Cup. Though a heartbreaking end, supporters knew an exciting era had dawned at the club.

Just weeks into the 1965/66 season Revie switched Giles into central midfield following an horrific injury to skipper Bobby Collins during a Fairs Cup tie against Torino. The astute Irishman's eye for a killer pass over any distance was soon apparent and he and Billy Bremner complemented each other brilliantly in midfield. Giles was not as volatile as Bremner, but possessed the same determination and will-to-win as his skipper, and in the heat of battle, Giles could be ruthless in his tackling. Orchestrating proceedings from the centre of the park Bremner and Giles became the most feared midfield partnership in the game.

Giles' ratio of goals from midfield was exceptional, scoring 115 in all competitions. A terrific striker of the ball, Giles hit double figures on five occasions during a season. Top scorer in 1966/67 with 18 goals, his most prolific campaign was 1969/70 when he scored 19. Although he was capable of striking from any distance, as he demonstrated superbly in a 5-0 win against Derby County in October 1973, Giles became renowned as a penalty expert. His accuracy and composure made him the ideal choice and he rarely missed. Succeeding Willie Bell, Giles scored his first penalty for Leeds against Birmingham City in November 1964. Ever-reliable, his best penalty haul was eight in 1969/70 and 1970/71, one short of Jack Milburn's record nine spot kicks in 1935/36. Giles would score 44 goals from penalties over nine seasons, more than any other Leeds player.

Dubbed the 'Penalty King' by the *Yorkshire Evening Post*, Giles came up trumps during crucial cup-ties, some of the most notable pressure spot kicks coming in European quarter-final matches against Bologna, Rangers, Standard Liege and Vitoria Setubal, and a League Cup semi-final clash against Derby County. On each occasion, Leeds won on aggregate. During the 1972/73 campaign Giles became only the second Leeds player to score a penalty in three consecutive league games (*v.* Sheffield United, West Brom and Ipswich Town), matching Milburn's feat in 1935/36.

When Don Revie became England manager in 1974, he recommended Giles as his successor at Leeds but the board ignored his advice. Within twelve months, Giles would also move on, but not before a final appearance at Wembley in the Charity Shield and another European Cup campaign, but the ultimate prize would elude Leeds.

Johnny Giles in action against Liverpool.

Throughout an incredible era, Giles helped Leeds win the First Division Championship and Fairs Cup twice, the FA Cup (notching a brace against Bristol Rovers and Cardiff City on the road to Wembley), League Cup and Charity Shield. He also played in three FA Cup finals, two European finals and was a First Division runner-up on five occasions. Despite the disappointments, Leeds won every domestic honour and were the team to beat every season.

His form naturally brought international recognition. After playing his first full international for the Republic of Ireland at eighteen, a record at the time, Giles went on to captain his country on many occasions, eventually winning 59 caps.

Within weeks of the European Cup final defeat in Paris, Giles began a successful spell as player-manager at West Brom. Guiding his players to promotion from the Second Division at the first attempt, he created one of the most attractive teams in the First Division before returning to Ireland in 1977 to manage Shamrock Rovers, where he won the FAI Cup. He then took up posts at Philadelphia Fury and Vancouver Whitecaps, before managing the Republic of Ireland and finally West Brom for a second spell.

Since his departure from the Hawthorns in 1985, Giles has developed a fresh career as a respected journalist, television pundit and an accomplished speaker on the after-dinner circuit. Eighth on the all-time list at Leeds United with 523 (+4 substitute) appearances, Johnny Giles was one of the greatest footballers to represent the club.

ARTHUR GRAHAM

Arthur Graham was an exciting player to watch when in full flow, and soon became a firm favourite with Leeds fans with his flashing runs down the left wing following his £125,000 transfer from Aberdeen during the summer of 1977.

Born in Glasgow on 26 October 1952, Graham made his name as a teenager, scoring one of Aberdeen's goals in a shock 3-1 success against Celtic in the Scottish League Cup final in 1970. However, after 230 appearances for the Dons, Graham accepted the challenge to move south when Jimmy Armfield offered him the opportunity. The move worked for both parties and Graham deservedly won a belated call up to the full Scotland side after a number of appearances for their Youth and Under-23 teams. He went on to win 10 caps for his country.

During his first season at Leeds, following his debut at Newcastle United and first goal for the club in a 2-2 draw at Derby County, a hat-trick during a 3-2 victory at Birmingham City quickly endeared him to supporters. Scoring 9 goals, he finished second-top scorer behind Ray Hankin as Armfield continued the process of bringing in fresh players to the side. Graham was a key player in the new set-up alongside new boys Tony Currie, Brian Flynn and Hankin, and in a reasonably successful campaign Leeds finished ninth and reached the League Cup semi-finals.

In 1978/79 Leeds reached another League Cup semi-final, agonisingly losing 3-2 against Southampton after leading in the first leg 2-0, and qualified for the UEFA Cup, despite two managerial changes! Unfortunately, his latter years at Leeds would be less successful as the team struggled for consistency. With the departure of strikers Hankin and John Hawley, goals were at a premium, even though Graham did his best with trebles against Maltese side Valetta and Wolves. His total of three hat-tricks would not be equalled for over twenty years.

An industrious player, Graham used his strength to muscle past opponents before cutting balls back from the byline. Willing to help in midfield to gain possession, Graham would often play on both flanks and down the centre to aid his team. This occurred more often in his latter years at the club as goals dried up.

In 1981/82 the team endured a traumatic season, which eventually resulted in relegation to the Second Division. In the clear out Graham helped a number of inexperienced

Arthur Graham goes close against Ipswich Town.

youngsters such as John Sheridan and Neil Aspin settle into the side as Eddie Gray began the difficult task of rebuilding the team.

Playing just one term, Graham looked to have rejuvenated his career when he joined Manchester United for £50,000, but after two seasons, he moved on again, this time to Bradford City where he ended his playing career in 1987. After holding a number of posts at Bradford, including coach, caretaker-manager and assistant manager, Graham has run soccer coaching clinics.

A loyal servant to Leeds United during a difficult period in the club's history, Arthur Graham made 259 (+1 substitute) appearances, scoring 47 goals. Serving five managers; he rarely let the team down and his popularity never diminished throughout his time at Elland Road.

Eddie Gray was one of the most sought after youngsters in the country when he joined Leeds United in January 1965. A prodigious talent, and blessed with unbelievable ball skills, Eddie was a majestic sight with his darting runs down the left flank. That he turned down his boyhood team Celtic for Leeds, like younger brother Frank some years later, says much for Don Revie's persuasive talents and vision for the club.

Born in Glasgow on 17 January 1948, Eddie scored on his league debut against Sheffield Wednesday on New Year's Day 1966, aged seventeen. By the end of the season, he had cemented his place in the first team and proceeded to tease, torment and bamboozle the best defenders in the First Division and Europe.

A member of the Leeds side that won the League Cup in 1968 and the First Division title a year later, Eddie reserved one of his greatest exhibitions of wing play for the 1970 FA Cup final. His virtuoso performance was even more remarkable due to the horrendous surface at Wembley that year following the Horse of the Year show and heavy rain. His efforts deservedly won him the Man of the Match award.

Following his incredible display at Wembley, the world was at his feet, but injuries were beginning to take their toll and luck was certainly against him, especially in Europe. Over the years in the Fairs Cup, injuries dashed his hopes of playing in a semi-final play-off against Real Zaragoza, the second leg of finals against Dynamo Zagreb and Ferencvaros, and in 1971, an awkward fall in the abandoned first leg of the Fairs Cup final against Juventus forced him to miss Leeds' eventual triumph.

As with his club career, injuries blighted Eddie's international career. Having represented Scotland at Schoolboy and Under-23 level, a full Scottish cap followed against England in the 1969 Home International Championships, but the 12 caps he eventually won were spread over seven seasons. One can only wonder what the world media would have written about Scotland at the 1974 World Cup finals if Eddie Gray had been fully fit.

Astonishingly, only once during the 1970s did Eddie play two-thirds of a league campaign, but thankfully he was able to take his place in many high-profile matches, especially during the club's treble bid in 1969/70 and he was present when Leeds celebrated their FA Cup triumph in 1972. Twelve months later he played in the cup final against Sunderland, before the European jinx struck again, forcing him to miss the 1973 European Cup Winners' Cup final. After coming though pre-season training, Eddie missed the majority of the 1973/74 season, before fighting his way back in time to make an appearance in the 1975 European Cup final.

Thereafter, Eddie finally experienced an injury-free run through the late 1970s. Playing for a number of managers, he once again thrilled supporters, scoring his only hat-trick against Leicester City in 1978. Brother Frank also scored, one of only four occasions the two did so for Leeds in a game. Although Leeds failed to win any silverware, they did reach three cup semi-finals and qualified for Europe in 1978/79.

Converting to left-back in 1980 added three years to his playing career, but within weeks of being voted Player of the Year in 1981/82, Eddie was planning for life in the Second Division with falling gates and little money. Blooding a number of promising apprentices during 1982/83, results began to improve; however, it was a thankless task.

After three years at the helm, his twenty-year association with the club ended in October 1985. Supporters were outraged, but he departed with dignity. A number of his youngsters,

EDDIE GRAY

Gray scores against Manchester City in the 1969 Charity Sheild.

most notably John Sheridan, Scott Sellars and Denis Irwin, went on to have fine careers, justifying his faith in them. Eddie had not only witnessed the club's rise from First Division upstarts to one of European football's most respected teams, but had also witnessed the club's decline to Second Division minnows. His days at Leeds, however, would not be quite over!

Resuming his playing career at non-league Whitby Town, Eddie finally retired in March 1986. Following a coaching role at Middlesbrough and managerial posts at Rochdale, Hull City and Whitby Town, Leeds United's prodigal son returned in 1995 as youth team coach. Under his tutelage the class of 1997 won the FA Youth Cup, the reserves clinched the Pontins League Division One title for the first time in sixty-one years and numerous youngsters that he nurtured such as Harry Kewell, Jonathan Woodgate, Paul Robinson and Alan Smith developed into international players.

Promoted to the first-team set-up in recent years, Eddie endured a roller-coaster ride as the finances of the club spiralled out of control. From Champions League contenders, Leeds were soon fighting for Premiership survival, and as a succession of managers departed, Eddie took the helm in a desperate bid to stave off relegation during the 2003/04 campaign. An impossible task, it surprised few supporters that his attempts failed, and when the inevitable occurred, his dignified departure demonstrated what the club meant to him.

Eddie will be remembered for his football skills, and rightly so, because he is the most naturally gifted player to represent Leeds United. In his distinctive style, Eddie could beat players for pace on the outside or inside. Although not renowned as a prolific goalscorer, among his 68 goals was a thirty-five-yard lob and an unbelievable solo effort against Burnley in 1970 that are acknowledged as among the greatest goals ever witnessed at Elland Road.

On his day, Eddie was unstoppable, and when on song no defender in the world was safe. Seventh on the all-time appearances list at Leeds having played 561 (+18 substitute) games, Eddie Gray was a sensational player.

FRANK GRAY —————————

Frank Gray, like elder brother Eddie, was a Celtic fanatic as a boy, but refused the overtures of thirty clubs to join Leeds United as an apprentice, signing professional forms in November 1971. This was a brave decision, as comparisons to Eddie would be made; placing additional pressure on young Frank. However, Leeds were at the height of their powers so his choice was understandable.

Born in Glasgow on 27 October 1954, Frank was an elegant player, a sublime passer of a ball and quick. Initially breaking into the first team as a substitute against Leicester City in 1973, within two months he scored on his full debut against Crystal Palace. His first campaign would end with an appearance in the European Cup Winners' Cup final against AC Milan.

Gray in action against Queens Park Rangers.

FRANK GRAY

A fringe player in 1973/74, midway through the 1974/75 campaign Jimmy Armfield gave Frank his opportunity at left-back, and he didn't disappoint domestically or in Europe against the likes of Barcelona in the European Cup. A member of the side that lost in the final to Bayern Munich, by the start of the new campaign the future centred on youngsters like Frank and once again he impressed everyone.

A terrific reader of the game, his unflappable temperament made him a natural penalty taker, converting his first against Derby County in March 1976. Frank shared this duty with Peter Lorimer for a number of seasons. Having represented Scotland at Schoolboy and Under-23 level, a full Scottish debut against Switzerland arrived in April 1976, though he would have to wait until 1978/79 to gain regular selection.

As Revie's legends moved on, the likes of Tony Currie, Brian Flynn and Arthur Graham arrived at the club. Although Leeds failed to win any silverware during the late 1970s, they did reach three cup semi-finals and managed to qualify for Europe again. In July 1979 Brian Clough tempted Frank to Nottingham Forest for a club-record fee of £500,000, and during a two-year spell, he enjoyed his most productive period as a player when Forest successfully defended the European Cup.

By 1981/82 Frank was back at Elland Road with former colleague Allan Clarke at the helm. Much had changed since his departure and in a traumatic league campaign Leeds lost their top-flight status. During the close season, as Leeds pondered life in the Second Division, Frank flew to Spain for the World Cup finals, appearing in all his country's games. In a distinguished career for Scotland, he won 32 caps.

His last years at Leeds would see his brother in charge. Frank added experience in either defence or midfield to the young team being assembled. However, by 1985/86, Frank needed a new challenge, and during brief spells helped Sunderland win promotion from the Third Division in 1987/88, and as player-assistant-manager at Darlington guided his team to the 1989/90 GM Vauxhall Conference title.

The Gray dynasty continued in 1995/96 when Frank's son Andy made his Leeds United debut. Remarkably, his fourth start, at the age of eighteen, would be in the League Cup final, but his stay would last only two seasons and 28 appearances. As for his father, Frank Gray should have achieved far more with his natural ability. Nevertheless, during a twelve-year career at Leeds, Frank made 396 (+9 substitute) appearances, giving consistently good performances season after season.

Jimmy Greenhoff represented Yorkshire Schools before serving his apprenticeship at Leeds United alongside the likes of Peter Lorimer and Eddie Gray. Although Leeds supporters only saw the formative years of Greenhoff's career, he made a valuable contribution to the development of Don Revie's side in the mid-1960s.

Born in Barnsley on 19 June 1946, Greenhoff was initially a right-sided midfield player and made his debut in 1963 against Swansea Town, but like many of Don Revie's talented youngsters had to be satisfied with sporadic appearances in the first team.

Waiting for an opportunity was frustrating, but when called upon Greenhoff impressed. He scored his first goal for the club in an exciting 3-2 win against Stoke City in 1964, before appearing in all three Fairs Cup semi-final clashes against Real Zaragoza during the club's first foray into Europe.

In 1966/67, Revie converted Greenhoff to striker. A natural footballer, his control, distribution, composure and ball-striking ability set him apart. Playing the target man, Greenhoff made 42 appearances in all competitions, scoring 10 goals, including a brace against Tottenham Hotspur in a 3-2 victory as Leeds finished fourth in the First Division. The youngster also helped Leeds reach the semi-finals of the FA Cup and notched an important goal against Valencia on the way to the Fairs Cup final. He played in the second leg against Dynamo Zagreb at Elland Road, but Leeds missed out 2-0 on aggregate.

When the new season began, there was speculation about a new striker, which proved correct. In September 1967, Mick Jones arrived for a club record £100,000 and Greenhoff's position in the team was in doubt, but with Jones cup-tied and Mike O'Grady struggling with injury Greenhoff stayed in the side, playing 54 games.

The 1967/68 campaign saw Leeds finally win a major honour, the Football League Cup. They also reached the semi-finals of the FA Cup and the Fairs Cup final for a second successive year and Greenhoff played his part. One of the few players to appear in every League Cup and Fairs Cup tie, Greenhoff was second top scorer with 16 goals. Among his goals was a hat-trick against Fulham and a brace in Leeds' 2-0 League Cup fifth-round win at Sunderland.

Greenhoff played in the delayed first leg of the Fairs Cup final against Ferencvaros and started the first three league fixtures of the new season; however, the next match at Ipswich saw the return of O'Grady. Within days, Greenhoff stunned supporters by joining Birmingham City for £70,000. It was difficult for Revie to hang on to all his talented players but it was still a sad day when this popular striker left.

After a three-year spell at Birmingham, Greenhoff enjoyed a fine career at Stoke City, winning the League Cup in 1972, before a £200,000 transfer took him to Manchester United in 1976, where in his third Wembley final he inadvertently scored the winning goal in the 1977 FA Cup final against Liverpool. Following a brief spell for Toronto Blizzard in Canada, he held management and coaching positions during the early 1980s at Crewe, Rochdale and Port Vale.

Unlucky not to add a full England cap to his 4 at Under-23 level, Jimmy Greenhoff scored 33 goals in 128 (+8 substitute) appearances for Leeds United and was an important squad member as they became a major force in the game.

Greenhoff waits to pounce in the 1968 League Cup Final.

GRENVILLE HAIR

Grenville Hair enjoyed a remarkable sixteen-year career throughout the 1950s and early 1960s at left-back for Leeds United, playing alongside some of the club's greatest players, including John Charles, Jack Charlton, Bobby Collins and Billy Bremner.

Born in Burton-upon-Trent on 16 November 1931, Hair's arrival at Elland Road from Newhall United in November 1948 coincided with a period of great change as manager Major Frank Buckley began the task of replacing players whose careers had ended during the Second World War. Naturally fit, the Major persuaded Hair to pursue a career in football rather than develop his prowess in athletics.

Leeds United c.1963, Grenville Hair, back row, second from left.

Buckley's success would be the club's gain but Hair would not make his Second Division debut until the latter stages of the 1950/51 campaign at Leicester City, as Jim Milburn's replacement, when Leeds finished fifth. The following term, Hair made the position his own and slowly the team developed as John Charles rewrote the club's goalscoring records. By 1955/56, Raich Carter was manager, and, timing their run to perfection, Leeds finished runners-up behind Sheffield Wednesday, a 4–1 victory at Hull City in the last game clinching promotion.

Neat, compact and a fine passer of the ball, Hair was now able to test himself against the likes of Stan Matthews, Stan Mortenson and Nat Lofthouse. An ever-present in the side for the third time in 1956/57, Hair was not out of place in such exalted company and deservedly won a place in the FA representative team that toured the West Indies in 1955, Nigeria and Ghana in 1958, and New Zealand in 1960.

Incredibly consistent, alongside Jimmy Dunn the two full-backs occupied the number two and three shirts for eight seasons, missing only 45 of 349 league and cup matches, and 32 of those appearances came in two campaigns! Without Charles, Leeds struggled for goals and after three years of relegation battles under Carter, Bill Lambton and Jack Taylor, Leeds found themselves back in the Second Division.

The 1960/61 campaign saw the appointment of Don Revie as player-manager. However, twelve months on it looked certain that Hair would be playing Third Division football, but Bobby Collins' arrival inspired a fine run that brought safety on the last day of the season. Astonishingly, during the club's fight for survival, Hair scored his only league goal for Leeds when he opened the scoring in a priceless 2–0 win against Middlesbrough.

Hair doubled his tally the following term in an FA Cup clash against Stoke City, and for two seasons witnessed the renaissance of the club as the likes of Gary Sprake, Paul Reaney and Norman Hunter came into the first team. However, by 1963/64 Hair was no longer an automatic choice when Willie Bell converted to left-back.

Hair played eight games of the successful promotion campaign as Leeds returned to the First Division, but during the close season joined Wellington Town as player-manager, before taking up a coaching position at Bradford City. In 1968 he was appointed manager, but after just one month in charge suffered a fatal heart attack during a training session at the age of just thirty-six.

A tremendous servant to Leeds United, Hair's speed, distribution, anticipation and tackling ability made him an indispensable member of the team in his 474 appearances. Only a few players have given their entire career to the club. Grenville Hair's loyalty was exemplary.

ERNIE HART

Ernie Hart was playing for Woodlands Wesleyans in Doncaster when Leeds United signed him in July 1920. During the club's inaugural campaign as a Football League club, the well-built teenager made his first-team debut against Boothtown in the FA Cup. Cementing his place in the side during the 1921/22 campaign, Hart would become one of the club's great central defenders during a sixteen-year career.

Born in Overseal on 3 January 1902, Hart made his debut against Stockport County and scored his first goal for Leeds in a 1-0 victory at Wolves in November 1922; Leeds ended the season seventh. The following term top-flight football arrived for the first time in the club's history. Promotion always seemed a possibility but the 1923/24 Second Division title was only secured in the penultimate game at home to Nelson. Hart scored one goal, which gained an important 1-0 win at Southampton.

Unfortunately, throughout their initial spell in the First Division, Leeds struggled. On occasion, games went according to plan such as a 6-0 win against Aston Villa on Christmas Day in 1924 when Hart grabbed his by-now customary seasonal goal. Relegation followed in 1926/27, Hart made only 5 appearances but he was back by December as Leeds mounted a charge for promotion under new boss Dick Ray. Seven consecutive wins followed, Hart scoring against Stoke City in a 5-1 win. Another spell saw no goals conceded in nine games, a club record. A defeat in Leeds' last home game cost the title but Leeds claimed top-flight status again as runners-up.

Among the elite in the First Division, Hart finally won England recognition when he made his full debut against Wales in November 1928. His skipper was Leeds teammate Willis Edwards, the first time two Leeds players had represented England in the same international. Hart and Edwards would line up against Ireland a year later when Leeds finished the 1929/30 campaign fifth, their highest finish since formation, a season also notable for a record 8-1 win against Crystal Palace in the FA Cup.

84

ERNIE HART

Life could hardly be better for the Leeds stopper but following relegation in 1930/31 Hart was dropped from the England set up. Always determined, he simply rolled up his sleeves and came back stronger. Leeds again bounced back at the first attempt, nine straight wins in the autumn confirming their desire. Two wins in the last ten cost the title, but the runners-up spot in 1931/32 was rarely in doubt. Hart scored once in a 4-1 win at Bury. A return to the First Division brought a call-up for England against Austria.

The next two league campaigns brought top-ten finishes, the highlight a club-record 8-0 win over Leicester City in 1934. Shortly after Hart played his last games for England, winning eight caps in all. Hart also represented the Football League and toured South Africa with the Football Association in 1929.

Thereafter, Leeds struggled at the wrong end of the table. Billy Hampson replaced Ray as manager during the latter stages of the 1934/35 season as the team flirted with relegation. Leeds survived following a late run when they lost one of their last six matches. Hart scored in the final game of the season during a thrilling 4-3 win against Tottenham Hotspur. His sixteenth goal for Leeds would be his final strike for the club and Hart would play just four more games for Leeds in 1935/36 before joining Mansfield for a two-year spell.

Following his retirement as a player, Hart managed Tunbridge Wells before scouting for Coventry City and Leeds prior to his death in 1954 aged fifty-two. A natural leader and motivator, Hart was an inspirational captain for Leeds. Respected around the country, he could tackle ferociously and gained a reputation for being 'hard', yet was sent off just once, which harshly resulted in him missing an FA tour to Italy and Switzerland.

Alongside Bill Menzies, Hart is the only Leeds United player to play in the Second Division Championship side and both promotion campaigns of the club's formative years. Hart played 472 games for Leeds, placing him twelfth on the all-time list for appearances.

During his time at Elland Road, Hart was part of a number of formidable partnerships in defence, the most notable being the half-back line of Edwards-Hart-Copping in the early 1930s. One can only speculate what opposition forwards would have made of this trio! Ernie Hart is justifiably a legend at Leeds United.

Paul Hart arrived at Leeds United following the shock departure of Gordon McQueen to Manchester United in January 1978. Jimmy Armfield had acted quickly to prise his former club's talented defender away for £300,000; Hart would go on to become a stalwart of the side, and eventually make his name as a promising coach.

Born in Manchester on 4 May 1953, Hart began his football career with Stockport County in 1970. The son of former Manchester City star Johnny Hart, a £25,000 fee took him to Blackpool in 1973, where he developed into a promising centre half.

Following his arrival at Elland Road, initially Hart struggled to adjust to top-flight football after a tough debut at Liverpool. The odd own goal didn't help his cause, but gradually he established himself in the side and became a commanding figure in defence. Brave and committed, Hart was superb in the air, effective in his tackling and took the simplest option when clearing his lines. Not many strikers relished playing against him. During a five-year

Hart (extreme right) waves to Leeds fans along with Trevor Cherry and David Harvey.

spell, Hart proved a sound investment whether playing alongside Paul Madeley, Trevor Cherry or Kenny Burns.

Despite taking instructions from three managers, Armfield, Jock Stein and Jimmy Adamson, in his first seven months, Hart's debut campaign would ultimately be his most successful. Missing few games, the season saw Leeds qualify for Europe after finishing the league campaign in fifth place, in addition to reaching the semi-finals of the League Cup, a tournament that brought a memorable goal for him against West Brom in a first-round replay. Indeed, his aerial power became an asset at set pieces, scoring seven goals that term. Sadly, his remaining years at Leeds would be hard graft.

Following the departure of strikers Ray Hankin and John Hawley during the 1979/80 season goals dried up, and although surviving the following term, with goals at a premium a traumatic 1981/82 campaign brought relegation, ending eighteen seasons of top-flight football. To Hart's credit, he helped a number of youngsters such as Neil Aspin, John Sheridan and Tommy Wright settle during the first Second Division campaign before enjoying brief spells at Nottingham Forest, Sheffield Wednesday, Birmingham City and Notts County.

At County, Hart extended his role to coaching, before taking on the responsibilities of management at Chesterfield. However, he reverted to coaching at two of his former clubs, Nottingham Forest and Leeds United. Back at Elland Road as Director of Youth Coaching, his youngsters won the FA Youth Cup in 1993 and 1997.

The class of 1993 included Noel Whelan and Jamie Forrester, but despite defeating Manchester United neither progressed like their counterparts at Old Trafford. However, the class of 1997 proved far more successful with Harry Kewell, Jonathan Woodgate, Paul Robinson and Stephen McPhail all making the grade. Following this success, it was somewhat surprising when he took on the challenge of developing the youth set up at Nottingham Forest again.

When David Platt departed from Forest to coach the England Under-21 side in 2001, Hart took over the managerial responsibilities at the City Ground on a full-time basis, until his departure last season. Now at Barnsley, his coaching skills will benefit players for some years to come. Regarding his time at Leeds United, during 223 games Paul Hart gave diligent service as both a player and inspirational coach.

Ian Harte joined Leeds United as an apprentice in 1995 and came through the ranks to become one of the club's most consistent performers of recent seasons. A talented left-back, he is also renowned as a dead-ball specialist.

Born in Drogheda on 31 August 1977, Harte lined up alongside his uncle, Gary Kelly, when he made his debut in a League Cup clash against Reading in 1996. Following George Graham's arrival as manager at the start of the 1996/97 season, it became apparent that the young Irishman didn't figure in the new boss' plans. Indeed Harte found it easier to get a game for the Republic of Ireland than his club!

However, when David O'Leary took the helm in 1998/99, Harte's fortunes changed for the better. With everyone getting an opportunity to impress, Harte held off a number of challengers to cement his place at left-back, and he played his part in O'Leary's revolution that saw Leeds reach the semi-finals of both the UEFA Cup and Champions League. Playing alongside Kelly, Lucas Radebe, Rio Ferdinand and Dominic Matteo, Leeds looked balanced and dangerous on the counter-attack.

A solid tackler and fine distributor of the ball, a key aspect to Harte's game is his prowess in not only making telling crosses on his frequent sorties forward but also his expertise when it comes to dead-ball situations. The club's regular penalty taker, Harte notched his first for the club in a 5-1 win at West Ham in May 1999. His ability from free-kicks both domestically and in Europe also made him one of the most dangerous exponents of the art.

Among numerous examples of Harte's wonder-strikes, arguably the best came in a Premiership clash at Tottenham Hotspur in 1999/00, against Deportivo La Coruna in the Champions League and Grasshoppers Zurich in the 2002/03 UEFA Cup. Although predominantly left-footed, Harte is also no slouch with his right foot, as he demonstrated with the winner against West Ham in October 1999.

Harte's 11 goals in 2000/01 included penalty strikes against Aston Villa, Tottenham, TSV Munich 1860 and Anderlecht, but was nevertheless a remarkable return. A club record for a left-back at Leeds in a season, it has not been bettered by any defender since the days of Jack Charlton when he top-scored with 12 goals as an emergency striker.

On the international stage, Harte made his Republic of Ireland debut against Croatia in 1996 and has become a regular member of the team. During the Republic's successful 2002 World Cup qualifying campaign, Harte scored some terrific goals and is likely to feature in future tournaments.

Since O'Leary's sacking, Ian Harte has struggled to rediscover his best form, and as a consequence his confidence has suffered. As off the field affairs and managerial shenanigans rocked the club, Harte's displays faltered alarmingly and it was no surprise that he lost his first-team place last season.

After Eddie Gray eventually took the helm in 2003, Harte returned but the club ultimately lost its battle against relegation. Now playing in Spain, whatever the future holds for this talented footballer, scoring 39 goals in 271 (+18 substitute) appearances over the past eight years, Ian Harte has made a lasting impression at Leeds United.

D avid Harvey made his Leeds United debut in a League Cup clash against West Brom in
October 1965. At seventeen, the teenager was at the start of a brilliant career but had
to be content with being Gary Sprake's understudy for seven years, playing 200 games for the
reserves and 38 for the first team. Harvey would go on to become one of the club's greatest
ever goalkeepers.

Born in Leeds on 7 February 1948, nobody could have blamed Harvey if he had decided
to join another side, where he would have undoubtedly been a first choice, but he didn't,
which says much for Don Revie's man-management skills in keeping fringe players happy.
His dedication would eventually pay off over a seventeen-year career.

Harvey was an incredibly hard trainer and put himself through the most punishing of
schedules to develop his skills. Whenever called upon, whatever the occasion, he never let
the team down. Notable appearances included Fairs Cup quarter-final clashes against Rangers
and Vitoria Setubal, a European Cup semi-final encounter versus Celtic at Hampden Park,
and a few days later an FA Cup final replay against Chelsea.

The turning point in his career followed a majestic display at Stoke City in April 1972. With the next fixture an FA Cup semi-final against Birmingham City, Revie had a massive decision to make. Should he retain Harvey or bring back Sprake, his more experienced keeper? On the morning of the match, Harvey won the vote.

One can only speculate what Revie's thought process was, but maybe he had finally decided that for all Sprake's natural ability he could not risk any more costly errors in high-profile matches. Harvey's calm display vindicated Revie's decision and in the final at Wembley a faultless performance in the triumph over Arsenal sealed his position as the number-one choice.

Composed, determined and courageous, Harvey soon won international recognition through his consistent performances for Leeds, making his Scottish debut against Denmark in November 1972. As for his first full campaign, after being stretchered off in an opening day defeat at Chelsea, he quickly recovered and helped Leeds reach the FA Cup and European Cup Winners' Cup finals. Although neither trophy would be won, Leeds began the 1973/74 league campaign with an incredible twenty-nine-game unbeaten run, and during a memorable campaign clinched the First Division title with a game to spare.

To cap a great season, Harvey played in the 1974 World Cup finals in West Germany. Though Scotland failed to get beyond the initial group stages, his sensational performances against Brazil, Yugoslavia and Zaire resulted in him winning an award for being the best goalkeeper in the tournament. Harvey would go on to win 16 caps for Scotland.

Following Don Revie's departure, Harvey missed the vital spot kick against Liverpool in the club's Charity Shield defeat at Wembley. After Jimmy Armfield replaced Brian Clough as manager, an horrific car crash mid-season ended his campaign prematurely. Thereafter, Harvey would remain first choice; bar the odd spell out through injury, during a decade that saw two more managers at the club.

It was always going to be an uphill task following the Revie era, but new stars such as Duncan McKenzie, Tony Currie and Arthur Graham did well in extremely difficult circumstances. Although Leeds failed to win any silverware during the late 1970s they reached three cup semi-finals and qualified for Europe once again.

Harvey decided to move on in 1980 and during a three-year spell played for the Canadian side Vancouver Whitecaps and Drogheda in Ireland. In 1983, at the request of Eddie Gray, he returned to Elland Road following the departure of John Lukic, to add vital experience to Gray's young team in the Second Division. Acting as skipper for two seasons, Harvey helped nurture the likes of John Sheridan, Tommy Wright and Scott Sellers, before finally severing links with the club in 1985 after 445 (+2 substitute) appearances. Following a brief spell with Bradford City he retired from the game.

It could not have been easy during the late 1960s and early 1970s for Harvey to watch Leeds season after season take on all-comers at home and abroad. That he did and waited for his opportunity says much about his character. Although Leeds United won six major honours during the Revie era, others escaped. David Harvey was a first-class goalkeeper and one can only wonder what additional trophies Leeds might have won had they benefited from his calming influence in the side earlier.

JIMMY FLOYD HASSELBAINK ——————

Jimmy Floyd Hasselbaink is one of the most controversial players to represent Leeds United in recent years. George Graham's 'hit-man' did not disappoint as a goalscorer; leading the line brilliantly during his two-year stay, but his departure angered supporters, despite the huge profit the club made.

Born in Paramambo on 27 March 1972, Hasselbaink arrived at Leeds from Portuguese side Boavista for £2m prior to the start of the 1997/98 season. After stabilising the club, Graham needed a target man at an affordable price and Hasselbaink fitted the bill, having scored 47 goals in two seasons for Boavista and Campomairorense.

Looking back at the Graham era, the Dutchman's endeavours for Leeds helped enormously at a time when goals were at a premium. Indeed, after the tedium of the 1996/97 season when the team scored just twenty-eight goals, their lowest ever total for a league campaign, the new term would prove very different.

Hasselbaink got off to a flyer with a debut strike against Arsenal before grabbing another in a classic at Elland Road when Leeds came from three goals down to defeat Derby County 4-3. The entertainment was at times sensational as Leeds beat Blackburn 4-0 and Derby 5-0 in successive matches, Hasselbaaink scoring in both encounters. Leeds would match their goals total from the previous season by Christmas and double it by the end of the campaign as the team achieved a UEFA Cup spot. Voted Player of the Year, Hasselbaink finished his debut season as top scorer with 22 goals.

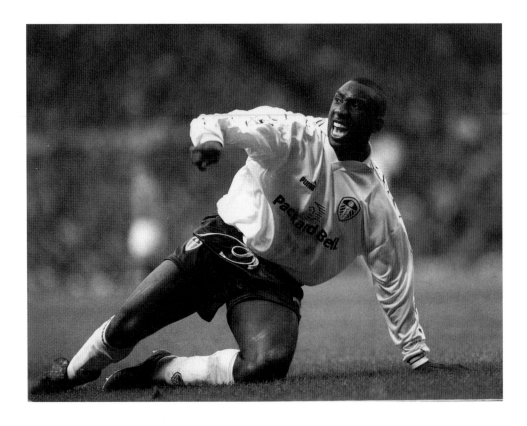

JIMMY FLOYD HASSELBAINK

'Jimmy' scores on his debut against Arsenal.

Selected for the Dutch World Cup squad in 1998, Hasselbaink played a minor role as Holland reached the semi-finals and certainly gained from the experience. Following David O'Leary's appointment as manager during the early stages of 1998/99, Hasselbaink was once again among the goals. Finishing top scorer with 20 goals, he scored in some memorable victories, notably notching twice in Leeds' 3-1 win at Liverpool.

On occasions though, his attitude was puzzling and he could frustrate fans, appearing to lose interest in a game. Yet he had the ability to turn a game in a flash, as he did with a brace in a 2-1 win at Aston Villa, and he struck some wonderful goals. Just as his first Leeds goal came against Arsenal so would his last, in the final home game of the season to hand the championship to Manchester United.

With another UEFA Cup campaign looming and many of O'Leary's youngsters established in the side, it was frustrating when Hasselbaink's contract talks floundered during the close season. Despite attempts to pacify his salary expectations he left the club acrimoniously, having scored 42 goals in 84 (+3 substitute) appearances, to Atletico Madrid for £12m. After one season in Spain, Hasselbaink returned to the Premier League with Chelsea.

Although he helped the Blues to an FA Cup Final appearance and the Champions League semi-finals, he joined Middlesborough during the close season where he teamed up with his successor at Elland Road, Mark Viduka.

A proven goalscorer for a number of years now, Hasselbaink's strength on the ball and shooting ability made him a handful for any defence. Like Cantona before him, Jimmy Floyd Hasselbaink will not be forgotten at Leeds United, but as with the Frenchman, for many supporters this former hero will be remembered for the wrong reasons.

GORDON HODGSON

Gordon Hodgson was in the twilight years of his career when he joined Leeds United in 1937. A first-rate striker, although his stay at the club was brief, Hodgson's performances and goalscoring exploits would astound Leeds supporters.

Born in Johannesburg on 16 April 1904, Hodgson made his name with Rurtenburg, Pretorian and Transvaal during the early 1920s before touring the United Kingdom with South Africa in 1925. During the trip he scored 15 goals and Liverpool quickly snapped him up. Hodgson went on to rewrite the club's scoring records. During 258 league appearances, he struck 233 goals, an incredible strike rate in any era.

Following a brief spell with Aston Villa, thirty-three-year-old Hodgson joined Leeds United for £1,500 towards the end of the 1936/37 season. With Leeds heading for relegation and main striker Arthur Hydes injured, Billy Hampson signed the veteran forward as an emergency replacement. He would not disappoint.

After a debut goal in a 7–1 defeat at Everton, his opening six games yielded one point. With seven games remaining, five were scheduled at Elland Road, which was fortunate because the team's away record that term, one win, one draw and 19 defeats, was the worst in the club's history. During a tense finale, Leeds won four home fixtures to secure their top-flight status with Hodgson scoring in victories against West Brom, Derby County and Sunderland.

Hodgson's last two campaigns for Leeds were less fraught as he finished top scorer in both terms, but three performances prior to the Second World War stood out. In 1937/38, he scored all Leeds' goals in a thrilling 4–4 draw with Everton prior to grabbing a hat-trick against Brentford in the last home match of the season. Nothing though could prepare supporters for the events on 1 October 1938 at Elland Road when Hodgson scored five goals against Leicester City in an 8–2 victory, a club record.

Although numerous Leeds United strikers have scored more goals than Hodgson, and Tom Jennings, Russell Wainscoat, Arthur Hydes, John Charles, John McCole, Allan Clarke, Peter

GORDON HODGSON

Lorimer and most recently Mark Viduka and Alan Smith all had four-goal performances, no-one has equalled Hodgson's stupendous feat. Some sixty-six years on, Billy McLeod of Leeds City is the only professional footballer in the city to match Hodgson's achievement.

The war years ended Hodgson's outstanding career, although he scored 14 goals in 33 wartime games for Leeds. By the time professional football resumed in 1947, Hodgson was Port Vale manager. He would remain in the post until his death in 1951 at the age of forty-seven.

A number of outstanding South African players have entertained Leeds supporters down the years, but before the likes of Albert Johanneson and Lucas Radebe, Gordon Hodgson paved the way. His goalscoring achievements compare favourably with the best strikers British football has produced and deservedly won him Football League representative honours and three England caps. Leeds United and Liverpool have always had the greatest of respect for each other. Scoring 53 goals in just 86 games, Gordon Hodgson was one of the early stars to instil this reverence.

Leeds United 1938/39. Back row: Hargreaves, Edwards, Toomey, Holley, Gadsby, Browne. Front row: Cochrane, Ainsley, Milburn, Hodgson, Stevenson.

TOM HOLLEY

Tom Holley played for Leeds United either side of the Second World War. A cultured and determined defender, following in the footsteps of his father, George Holley, who played for Wolves, Sunderland and England, was no easy task, but Tom developed into a valued member of the side at Elland Road.

Born in Wolverhampton on 15 November 1913, Holley junior was on his hometown club's books as a schoolboy prior to joining Sunderland as an apprentice but failed to make it into the first XI. Thereafter he took a different road to his father, although his dad was trainer at Barnsley when he gained his first professional contract in 1933.

Developing into a promising centre half, Leeds United manager Billy Hampson paid £3,750 for his services in July 1936. His first season at Elland Road saw Leeds battling against relegation. Holley made his debut against Stoke City before playing in a 7-1 defeat at Everton. His seventh appearance in a fraught campaign came in the last match at home to Portsmouth when Leeds' 3-1 success preserved their First Division status.

In 1937/38 Holley established himself in the first team as Leeds climbed to second place in the First Division at Christmas. Unfortunately, Leeds slipped to ninth following five wins after the New Year. The final season before the Second World War saw Leeds finish comfortably in mid-table, the highlight an 8-2 win over Leicester City, a result not bettered until 1967 when Revie's Leeds beat Spora Luxembourg 9-0.

When league football resumed after the war Holley, who played 104 wartime games for Leeds, returned to Elland Road along with a number of his former colleagues, but age had caught up with several key players.

As the 1946/47 campaign developed it told on their fitness. Leeds had their worst season ever, winning just six matches, and relegation was confirmed long before the final games. Former legend Willis Edwards replaced Hampson before the end of the campaign, but when Leeds finished the 1947/48 season in eighteenth place, their lowest placing since formation, the board decided to act and appointed Major Frank Buckley as the new boss.

Nearing the end of his playing days, Holley started a career with the *Yorkshire Evening Post* as a journalist. He would play one more season for Leeds, scoring his only goal for the club in a 3-2 defeat against West Ham on Christmas Day 1948. Holley's successor was teenage sensation John Charles and the budding journalist would write many column inches over the coming years about the up-and-coming star for the *Yorkshire Evening Post* and *Sunday People*. A contributor to the Leeds United match day programme in the mid-1970s, Holley spent much of his retirement in Spain, returning home to Yorkshire in 1989 prior to his death in 1992.

Tom Holley was a dedicated player for Leeds United during a difficult era. Making 169 appearances, Holley gave his all in every game and rarely let the team down, which says a lot about his capabilities as a footballer.

NORMAN HUNTER

Norman Hunter was renowned during the 1960s and 1970s as one of the 'hard' men of the game alongside the likes of Ron Harris of Chelsea, Dave Mackay of Spurs and Nobby Stiles of Manchester United. A ferocious tackler and a colossus in defence, Hunter was an integral part of Don Revie's legendary team and one of the great personalities of British football.

Born in Eighton Banks, County Durham on 24 October 1943, Hunter joined Leeds as an apprentice in November 1960. Early on in the 1962/63 season, Revie decided to introduce the first of his talented youngsters and Hunter was one of those chosen when Leeds faced Swansea Town in September 1962. By the end of the campaign, Hunter was a fixture in the side and even scored his first goals for the club, against Middlesbrough and Charlton Athletic, where he scored the winning goal in a 2-1 win.

One of the pre-season favourites for promotion in 1963/64, Leeds clinched the title in the final game of the season. Hunter was the only ever-present in the side and again notched two goals, against Middlesbrough and Swindon Town. Following the Second Division title success, Hunter experienced all the highs and lows of the Revie era as Leeds took on all comers domestically and in Europe.

The only Leeds player to appear in every major cup final Leeds played between 1965 and 1975, Hunter was ever-present during both First Division Championship triumphs. He won the Fairs Cup twice, and FA Cup, League Cup and Charity Shield winners' medals, and featured in Fairs Cup, European Cup Winners' Cup, European Cup finals, and three FA Cup finals. Hunter was also a regular in the side that finished First Division runners-up on no fewer than five occasions during an amazing era.

Over the years, Hunter's level of consistency was phenomenal and his value to the team immeasurable. However, his tackling ability became his trademark and you had to feel sympathy for a forward challenging him for a fifty–fifty ball. At times, some challenges looked brutal but he would never aim to hurt another player, though AC Milan pushed him to the limit in 1973! Naturally, he did have the odd spat on the pitch, most notably with Francis Lee in his Derby County days, when the pair were sent off.

The club's Player of the Year in 1971 and PFA Player of the Year in 1973, Hunter is arguably the fiercest competitor to represent Leeds but there was much more to his game than just being an effective stopper. Quick, totally committed and blessed with great positional awareness, Hunter could slice a defence open with a long raking pass, play his way out of defence with consummate ease, support the attack brilliantly (as he demonstrated against Southampton in 1972 when making a goal for Charlton) and pack a thunderous shot, as numerous goalkeepers found out.

Of his 21 goals for Leeds, Hunter's only strike in the FA Cup came in the infamous 3-2 defeat at Colchester United in 1971. He enjoyed his most prolific season in 1965/66, notching five goals, including the only goal of the season's opener against Sunderland and a brace against West Ham in a 5-0 win.

Developing a superb understanding alongside Jack Charlton, Paul Reaney and Willie Bell (replaced by Terry Cooper in 1967), Hunter was part of a defensive unit that could handle the best strikers around. During his final three seasons at Leeds, Hunter formed a fine partnership alongside Gordon McQueen in the centre of defence. However, after sixteen years at Elland Road Hunter was one of the first of Revie's legends to depart, joining Bristol City in 1976.

After a three-year spell, Hunter joined Barnsley as player-coach, becoming manager when Allan Clarke departed to Leeds in 1980. Retiring as a player, Hunter guided the Tykes to promotion in his first season at the helm prior to holding posts at West Brom, Rotherham, Leeds and Bradford City.

For England, having won 3 caps for the Under-23s, Hunter made history on his full debut against Spain, when he became the first England player to be capped as a substitute. Playing in defence or occasionally midfield, he won 28 full caps, scoring twice. In many ways, Hunter was unlucky because he competed for a place against the great Bobby Moore, which meant he won far fewer caps than his ability deserved.

Nevertheless, a member of the 1966 and 1970 World Cup squads, playing in the classic quarter-final clash with West Germany, Hunter gave everything for his country. Of his international appearances, unfortunately the most memorable one was an infamous clash against Poland in 1973. The Polish goal was a nightmare, but the media treated him harshly for his missed tackle in the build up. Hunter also made 6 appearances for the Football League and played in the Common Market Celebration match in 1973.

In recent years, this popular character has become a regular on the after-dinner circuit and an accomplished football pundit on BBC Radio Leeds. Playing more European ties than any other Leeds player (78); Hunter made 724 (+2 substitute) appearances for Leeds with only Bremner, Charlton and Reaney ahead of him on the all-time list. In an astonishing career, after making his debut in 1962, Hunter featured in 439 of 462 league games. A magnificent footballer, Norman 'Bites yer Legs' Hunter was a tremendous servant and a legend at Leeds United.

ARTHUR HYDES

Leeds United 1935/36. Hydes is seated third from the right.

Arthur Hydes terrorised defences for Leeds United. Hydes was a centre forward of some repute and one of the most clinical finishers around during the 1930s.

Born in Barnsley on 24 November 1911, Hydes' failed to impress during a trial at Southport, but by the end of the 1929/30 campaign was spotted by Leeds scouts playing for Ardsley Recreation, and manager Dick Ray was quick to sign him.

Having just finished fifth, optimism was high at Leeds but inconsistent form in 1930/31 resulted in relegation to the Second Division. Breaking into the side was always going to be difficult but when Hydes got an opportunity he took it, scoring on his first-team debut in an FA Cup clash against Huddersfield Town and on his league debut against Blackburn Rovers.

The 1931/32 campaign saw Leeds make an immediate return to top-flight football as Second Division runners-up, but again Hydes found himself on the periphery. The next season, however, Hydes joined Charlie Keetley and Billy Furness in attack and during a memorable campaign outgunned his colleagues, top scoring with 20 goals, including his first Leeds hat-trick during a 3-0 victory against Newcastle United in the FA Cup.

Hydes was in his prime and opened the 1933/34 campaign by scoring in five of the opening six games. His 9 goals included four against Middlesbrough in a 5-2 win, making him only the third player in the club's history to record such a feat. His third treble for Leeds in less than a year came at home to Blackburn before an injury at Newcastle sidelined him for ten months. Nevertheless, Hydes ended the season as top scorer with 16 goals from his 19 appearances.

Fighting back to fitness after a ten-month absence, Hydes scored in a 2-0 win against Everton and as in the previous campaign grabbed a hat-trick against Blackburn. He also scored a brace in eight further games, but his goals could not prevent Leeds slipping deeper into trouble. Inconsistency cost Ray his job before new boss Billy Hampson guided Leeds to safety. For a third successive season, Hydes finished top scorer, striking 22 goals in 30 games.

Sadly, much of the next two seasons for Hydes would be blighted by injury, yet his 19 league appearances in 1936/37 enabled him to finish the campaign as top scorer for a fourth time, the first player to do so, before ending his career with brief spells at Newport County and Exeter either side of the Second World War.

Arthur Hydes scored 82 goals in 137 appearances for Leeds United, but was unable to display his awesome talent for a sustained period due to injuries. Fortunately, statistics tell the story of this tremendous striker. Top scorer four times in five seasons with 65 goals in 107 appearances, Hydes' strike rate was phenomenal. Fast, determined and a natural goal poacher, few strikers matched Hydes' exploits during his heyday.

Tom Jennings was one of the most clinical finishers around in the 1920s and the first 'top-class' striker to play for Leeds United. His final tally of 117 goals would have been far greater had he not suffered from persistent injuries.

Born in Strathaven on 8 March 1902, Jennings' began his career at Raith Rovers in 1921 and survived a shipwreck on the way to the Canary Islands, but after his debut for Leeds against Sheffield United in March 1925, he made an immediate impact in his first full season, top scoring with 26 goals. Unfortunately, during the club's initial First Division spell the team struggled, finishing in the bottom four each season, and but for a 4-1 win on the last day of the 1925/26 season when Jennings grabbed a brace, would have been relegated. The following term the inevitable did happen, despite Jennings scoring 35 goals, more than half the team's total.

The season may have ended in disappointment for Leeds, but for Jennings it had been a sensational campaign. His club-record haul included four hat-tricks, and nineteen of his goals came in nine games, including eleven in consecutive matches against Arsenal (3) Liverpool (4) and Blackburn (4). Eight decades on, two records still stand as John Charles scored five hat-tricks and 42 league goals in 1953/54. Records are made to be broken but Jennings' three consecutive hat-tricks could well stand for all time.

Back in the Second Division, Dick Ray was appointed manager and promotion was rarely in doubt. Jennings, Russell Wainscoat, Charlie Keetley and John White terrorised defences, scoring seventy-eight league goals. Two unbeaten runs underpinned the campaign; the first brought seven consecutive victories, Jennings scoring in a 5-0 win versus Chelsea (4), and a brace against Stoke City and Port Vale. A defeat in the last home game to Manchester City cost the title, but Leeds deservedly finished runners-up. Jennings finished joint-top scorer with White, but Jennings' 21 goals came in 26 games compared to White's 41, a remarkable rate.

Unfortunately, injuries were limiting the maestro's appearances, but Leeds did have a new star emerging in Keetley. Bizarrely, the five games they played together in 1928/29 brought no victories. Indeed the defeats against Huddersfield 6-1, West Ham 8-2 and Burnley 5-0 were the heaviest of the season. One can only speculate what the two in their prime could have achieved.

Leeds surprised many teams by ending the 1929/30 campaign in fifth place, their highest finish since formation. It was also a season notable for a record 8-1 win in the FA Cup against Crystal Palace, Jennings scoring twice. There was genuine belief that Leeds could challenge for the title, but the 1930/31 season turned into a nightmare not only for Leeds but also for the injury-prone Jennings.

Occasionally, Leeds could be brilliant but the majority of the campaign was a relegation battle, lost on the last day of the season. Injuries had caught up with Jennings; and with

TOM JENNINGS

Keetley and Furness the first-choice strikers, Leeds' top striker at the time joined Chester during the close season, where he would score 31 goals in his first season! It is interesting to note that in Jennings' last three campaigns for Leeds, despite his absence for long periods, he scored 30 goals in his 50 appearances.

Following his retirement, Jennings managed Bangor City and Third Lanark but it is his years at Leeds that provided him with his most memorable days in football. One of Arthur Fairclough's most astute signings, bar injuries he would undoubtedly have played for Scotland; the closest Jennings came was a trial match in 1928.

Playing 174 matches for Leeds United, Jennings is the fourth-highest scorer in the club's history, behind Peter Lorimer, John Charles and Allan Clarke, and his 37 goals in all competitions during 1926/27 is still the third highest in a season, surpassed only by the legendary Charles. The first player in the club's history to score four goals in a game, Tom Jennings' strike rate compares favourably with the very best to have represented the club and his long-standing records at Leeds are testament to his prowess.

ALBERT JOHANNESON ————————

Albert Johanneson made an enormous contribution to Leeds United's development during the early years of Don Revie's reign as manager. Johanneson's efforts were all the more remarkable because he was treated as a second-class citizen in South Africa, and in England he played in an era when he had to overcome racist taunts from fans, and opponents at times, because he was a black footballer.

Born in Johannesburg on 13 March 1940, Johanneson arrived at Leeds in April 1961. On the football field, Johanneson made an immediate impact on his debut by creating a goal for Jack Charlton against Swansea Town. However, after starting the 1961/62 season in the side, he lost his place before returning for the final five games. The campaign almost brought relegation but the arrival of Bobby Collins brought stability and safety arrived in the last match when Johanneson scored the opening goal in a 3-0 win at Newcastle United.

As youngsters came into the side the following term, Revie's mix of youth and experience blended perfectly. Leeds began the 1963/64 campaign confidently and headed the table for much of the season. Promotion was secured with two games to go, the Second Division title in the last game at Charlton Athletic. Affectionately dubbed the 'Black Flash', Johanneson finished joint-top scorer with 13 goals, including a peach of a goal against Newcastle in a crucial 2-1 victory during the Easter fixtures.

Under Collins, Leeds took the First Division by storm and astounded everyone by almost claiming the double. Johanneson celebrated his top-flight debut with the opening goal of the season during a 2-1 victory at Aston Villa. A threat whenever in possession, he quickly became a marked man. His one weakness was self-confidence, which affected some performances, but when on song Johanneson could destroy any full-back in the game.

Blessed with blistering pace, skill on the ball and a terrific shot, Johanneson caused havoc for defences with his dazzling runs and crosses from the left flank. One of the most dangerous wingers around, Johanneson was a revelation, scoring terrific goals, including a brace against Everton in a 4-1 win, and on a historical note he became the first black player to appear in an FA Cup final at Wembley when Leeds lost to Liverpool in 1965.

Johanneson's reputation meant he had to put up with some horrendous challenges over the coming seasons, resulting in various injuries that kept him out of the team for long periods. Nevertheless, he provided some memorable moments, especially in the Fairs Cup with a crucial goal in a semi-final clash against Real Zaragoza, and hat-tricks against DWS Amsterdam and Spora Luxembourg.

Eddie Gray's development meant fewer opportunities for Johanneson, and in his last game for Leeds, Gray scored a virtuoso goal against Burnley. At the end of the 1969/70 campaign, Johanneson joined York City, where he would end his playing career. Tragically, he developed an addiction to drink and despite support from friends and former colleagues became a recluse before his death in 1995.

Albert Johanneson scored 67 goals in 197 (+3 substitute) appearances for Leeds and was one of the most talented wingers around in his heyday. However, his influence went far beyond scoring goals for Leeds United. History will show that this extraordinary individual's greatest legacy was paving the way for future South African footballers such as Lucas Radebe to follow in his footsteps on the world stage.

Mick Jones against Sheffield Wednesday.

M ick Jones joined Leeds United in September 1967 for a club-record fee of £100,000. Totally unselfish, Jones grabbed his share of goals but it was his non-stop running for the benefit of the team that made him invaluable, a handful for defenders and a vital member of Don Revie's legendary side.

Born in Worksop on 24 April 1945, as a youngster Jones once scored fourteen goals in a match for his school team! After playing for Worksop and Rotherham Boys, he joined Sheffield United in 1962 at seventeen and during five years scored 63 goals in 149 appearances. Capped at Under-23 level, he made two appearances for the full England team on a summer tour of Scandinavia in 1965.

Jones' move to Leeds gave Revie's team a cutting edge. Following his debut against Leicester City, Jones quickly established himself in the side and he notched his first Leeds goal in his European bow against Spora Luxembourg. Leeds' 9-0 win was a club record at the time. A niggling injury meant a spell on the sidelines but he was soon proving his potential on his return with a fine goal against Wolves and a brace in a comprehensive 5-0 victory at Fulham.

Jones duly claimed his first major honour when he scored the only goal of the delayed Fairs Cup final against Ferencvaros at the start of the 1968/69 season. In the League, after scoring in the opening three games of the season, he ended his first full campaign top scorer with 14 goals as Leeds claimed the First Division title. Notable winners came against Liverpool, Sunderland and QPR, and two important strikes during the run-in at Arsenal and at home to Leicester City.

During the close season, Allan Clarke arrived at the club, which proved a master stroke as Jones now had the perfect foil for his talents. From their first game together in the Charity Shield against Manchester City, the Clarke-Jones partnership clicked. The duo would become renowned at home and abroad as one of the finest in Europe, and with Peter Lorimer and Eddie Gray supporting from the flanks as an attacking force, no team was safe.

Jones used his strength to maximum effect in every game, whether shielding the ball, chasing lost causes or causing havoc in the penalty area before laying off a ball for his colleagues. He was also superb in the air and packed a fine shot. Enjoying his most prolific season in 1969/70, Jones opened the campaign with a brilliant headed winner at Manchester United and scored his first Leeds hat-trick in a club record 10-0 win against Lyn Oslo in the European Cup.

By the end of a titanic campaign, the strike duo had scored 26 goals apiece as Leeds chased the treble. However, in a traumatic finale, Leeds ended the season with nothing, despite Jones giving Leeds the lead in both the FA Cup final and replay against Chelsea. The season brought Jones his third England cap, against Holland in 1970, but mysteriously the best partnership domestically never played together on the international stage.

Over the next four seasons 'Jonah' was at his peak as Leeds won the FA Cup, Jones crossing the ball for Clarke's winner, another Fairs Cup title and a second First Division crown, when again he top scored with 14 goals. Among some distinguished performances in 1973/74, Jones scored the only goal of a tight encounter with Liverpool, a brace against West Ham and the opener in a 2-0 win at Old Trafford. Jones helped Leeds reach three FA Cup finals, two Fairs Cup Finals and a European Cup Winners' Cup final and played his part as Leeds finished runners-up in the First Division on three occasions.

Mick Jones calmly moves in to slot home his second in United's 2-0 victory against Crystal Palace.

As the target man, Jones endured cynical punishment and tragically, a bad knee injury midway through the second title campaign ultimately ended his playing career in October 1975. Indeed, his final game for Leeds was the penultimate match of the 1974 campaign against Ipswich Town, a game that ultimately clinched the title.

The abiding memory of Mick Jones for many Leeds United supporters is Wembley 1972, when, with his arm in a sling, he walked in agony across the pitch determined to receive his winners' medal from the Queen in the Royal Box. The seventh-highest scorer for the club with 111 goals in 308 (+5 substitute) appearances, Jones was top scorer on three occasions, and arguably, his most memorable display was when he grabbed a hat-trick against Manchester United in 1972, only the second Leeds player to do so. The club's Player of the Year in his final season, Jones was the ideal target man.

oe Jordan began his career at Morton in 1968. Recommended to Leeds United by his
veteran teammate and former Leeds legend Bobby Collins, Don Revie signed the raw
teenage striker for £15,000 in October 1970. Jordan would terrorise the best defenders in
world football.

Born in Carluke, Lanarkshire on 15 December 1951, initially Jordan replaced Mick Jones or
Allan Clarke when either was injured, but such was his progress Rod Belfitt departed. The
youngster made his bow as a subsitute at Arsenal before scoring on his full Leeds debut against
Barcelona in a Fairs Cup play-off match in 1971 and over the next three seasons, during
sporadic runs in the first team, got used to more crucial matches, playing in the semi-final and
final of the European Cup Winners' Cup in 1973.

Jordan in action
against Arsenal.

JOE JORDAN

Jordan finally got his break in 1973/74 and helped Leeds secure the First Division title. Never letting the team down, he scored some crucial goals, notably a late equaliser at Birmingham City and two great strikes against Arsenal.

Already a Scottish international, Jordan became a national hero in October 1973 when he scored a brilliant goal against Czechoslovakia to book his country's place at the 1974 World Cup finals. Though Scotland failed to get beyond the initial group stages, Jordan played superbly, scoring against Zaire and Yugoslavia.

Following Don Revie's departure, Jordan began the 1974/75 season in the first team. Playing against Liverpool in the Charity Shield at Wembley, Jordan led the line as Leeds reached the European Cup final. As the likes of Billy Bremner, Norman Hunter, Jones and Johnny Giles moved on, Jimmy Armfield introduced Duncan McKenzie and Tony Currie alongside Jordan, Gordon McQueen and Frank Gray, and during the mid-1970s Leeds were unlucky not to win silverware; falling at the semi-finals of the FA Cup in 1977.

A regular for club and country, Jordan was utterly fearless and an awesome sight in full flow, his direct running intimidating opponents. Tremendously strong in the air, he excelled at laying a ball off or shielding a ball until a colleague was better placed. Defenders wound him up, but Jordan was capable of looking after himself!

A few months into the 1977/78 campaign, Jordan shocked Leeds supporters by joining arch-rivals Manchester United for a club-record fee of £350,000. It was a massive blow to Leeds, but not to Jordan, who, after appearing in the 1978 World Cup finals, when he again scored, enhanced his reputation during three seasons at Old Trafford, helping them to the 1979 FA Cup final.

In 1981, Jordan joined Italian giants AC Milan, before playing in a third World Cup. Scoring against New Zealand made him the only Scot to score in three consecutive finals. Jordan gained 52 caps for his country. Following a season at Verona, this cracking old-fashioned-style centre forward joined Southampton for £100,000 in 1984.

Joining Bristol City, Jordan helped them win the Freight Rover Trophy in 1986. Appointed player-manager, he steered City to a League Cup semi-final in 1988/89 and promotion to the Second Division the following year. Since then, he has held a number of managerial and coaching posts at Hearts, Celtic, Stoke City, Bristol City again, Northern Ireland and Huddersfield Town.

For all his successes, Joe Jordan played some of his best football at Leeds United. Scoring 48 goals in 183 (+38 substitute) appearances, Jordan was top scorer in 1976/77, including winning strikes against Arsenal, Everton, Sunderland and Derby County and the perfect replacement for Mick Jones. Playing more games for Leeds than for his future clubs, Leeds supporters saw the development of a fantastic talent.

CHARLIE KEETLEY

Charlie Keetley was a phenomenal striker for Leeds United during the late 1920s and early part of the following decade. Following legendary striker Tom Jennings was no easy task, but Keetley proved just as clinical, setting records galore.

Born in Derby on 10 March 1906, Keetley was one of twelve children (eleven brothers and a sister) and was destined to become a footballer. Nine brothers played for local team Victoria Ironworks, five brothers went on to play professional football. Arthur played for Spurs, Frank, Harold, Joe and Tom played for Doncaster Rovers, Frank also played for Derby County. Another brother, Albert, played for Burton United. As for Charlie, during the 1926/27 season he scored 80 goals for non-league Alvaston & Boulton. Leeds scouts witnessed his progress and Dick Ray signed him in July 1927.

Keetley made an immediate impact at Leeds, scoring seven goals against Bolton Wanderers in a Central League fixture, before finally breaking into the first team during the second half of the 1927/28 league campaign. Scoring on his debut against South Shields, Keetley grabbed goals in his next three games, including a hat-trick against Bristol City. Two more trebles followed against Notts County and Clapton Orient, taking this incredible talent's total to 16 goals in just 18 appearances!

It was some introduction and Keetley's efforts were a major reason for the club's promotion back to the First Division at the first attempt when, along with Jennings, Russell Wainscoat and John White, Leeds terrorised defences, scoring seventy-eight league goals.

A Keetley hat-trick on the opening day of the 1928/29 season against Aston Villa demonstrated top-flight football held no fears for the youngster, and more trebles against Leicester City and Everton helped Leeds finish mid-table. Leeds' latest scoring machine was

PLAYER'S CIGARETTES.

top scorer with 20 goals. Keetley partnered Jennings for five games, but far from being a dream partnership, defeats against Huddersfield 6-1, West Ham 8-2 and Burnley 5-0 were the heaviest of the season!

Leeds surprised many teams by finishing the 1929/30 First Division campaign fifth, their highest position since formation. Keetley missed much of the season through injury but notched 10 goals in 9 starts during the latter stages, including a trademark hat-trick against Arsenal. The new term saw Keetley finish top scorer with 16 goals, but the 1930/31 campaign was a disaster for the club. Despite thumping wins against Blackpool 7-3, Middlesbrough 7-0 and Manchester United 5-0, there would be inconsistent spells, with relegation confirmed on the last day of the season.

For the second time in four years, Keetley was chasing promotion, but success was rarely in doubt throughout 1931/32. Keetley scored yet another treble, against Oldham Athletic, during a run of nine consecutive wins in the autumn, and Leeds should have won the title but a poor run near the end dashed the team's hopes.

Immensely strong and blessed with a rocket shot, Keetley was in imperious form throughout the campaign, scoring a brace against Chesterfield, Nottingham Forest, Bradford and Notts County, and a crucial strike against Southampton in the penultimate game at Elland Road that guaranteed promotion. Keetley finished top scorer with 23 goals.

Back in the First Division, Leeds finished in the top-ten for the next two campaigns, but Keetley was picking up injuries and missed more than half the league games. He was still scoring his quota of goals, including a hat-trick against Wolves a day after his twenty-seventh birthday, but with Arthur Hydes being first-choice centre forward, Keetley moved on, playing for Bradford City and Reading before retiring from the game in 1935.

Eighth-highest scorer for Leeds United, during six years Keetley plundered 110 goals in 169 appearances, and like Jennings before him created some unbelievable scoring records. Scoring ten hat-tricks, Keetley is second only to John Charles with 11. Both players scored three hat-tricks in a season; but even Charles failed to notch a hat-trick in six successive seasons (1927/28 to 1932/33)! Top scorer on three occasions, Charlie Keetley, who died in 1979, was one of the club's great goalscorers of the post-war era.

Gary Kelly joined Leeds United in July 1991 from Home Farm in Dublin. Over thirteen years he has witnessed the club's rise to the summit of British football and fall from grace following 2003/04's relegation from the Premier League. One of only two players, John Lukic being the other, to make 400 appearances for the club since the Don Revie era, Kelly has been a central figure as both a player and captain.

Born in Drogheda on 9 July 1974, Kelly is the youngest of thirteen children. Making his debut as a striker against Scunthorpe United in a League Cup clash in October 1991 at just seventeen, he failed to break into the first team on a regular basis. However, fate helped the youngster when Kelly converted to right-back at manager Howard Wilkinson's suggestion due to an injury crisis.

Throughout 1993/94 Kelly was a sensation. Quick, tenacious and intelligent, the young Irishman learned his defensive duties and utilised his pace to support the forwards with his overlapping runs down the right flank. Incredibly, by the end of his first full season; Kelly had cemented a place in the first team, made his international debut against Russia and played in the World Cup finals!

An ever-present the following term, Kelly enhanced his reputation as Leeds qualified for the UEFA Cup in 1994/95 and reached the League Cup final the following term. Following Wilkinson's departure in September 1996, Kelly lost his place in the side, but fought his way back to play a key role in the team's development under George Graham. Kelly also scored his first goal for the club in a 2-0 win at Southampton.

After helping Leeds qualify for the UEFA Cup in 1997/98, a nasty injury prior to the start of the next campaign resulted in Kelly missing an entire season as David O'Leary blooded a

crop of young players. The signing of Danny Mills kept Kelly on the bench at the start of 1999/00, but Mills' inconsistency enabled Kelly to re-establish himself in the side. During a memorable season, with skipper Lucas Radebe ruled out through injury, Kelly led Leeds to the semi-finals of the UEFA Cup and third place in the Premiership.

The following campaign, Kelly's injury jinx struck again as Leeds stunned the football world by reaching the semi-finals of the Champions League. In recent seasons, Kelly has demonstrated his versatility by filling in at centre-back and midfield, and even added to his goals tally with a terrific free-kick against Crystal Palace during an FA Cup clash in 2003, taking his total to four! Granted a testimonial, Kelly donated the proceeds to charity.

On the international scene, Kelly represented his country for many years and helped them qualify for the 2002 World Cup, though his sending off in the last fixture against Holland made life difficult for his teammates. Announcing his international retirement in 2003, Kelly won 52 caps, scoring twice.

Gary Kelly is the only player to serve Leeds United throughout the Premiership era, and with the club entering a new phase, after 402 (+15 substitute) appearances to the end of 2003/04, he is very much a part of the club's renaissance. Kelly has been a tremendous servant when his loyalty and commitment have stood out. In the modern era, it could well be some time before we find another player as dedicated.

ERIC KERFOOT

Eric Kerfoot was playing non-league football when Leeds United signed him from Stalybridge Celtic in December 1949. Eventually captaining the club, Kerfoot would become one of the most consistent players at Leeds, experiencing both promotion and relegation during a decade at Elland Road.

Born in Ashton-under-Lyne on 31 July 1924, Kerfoot at twenty-five was relatively old to be joining the professional ranks but he had a reputation as one of the best wing halves outside the Football League and his £3,000 transfer fee would prove a sound investment by Major Frank Buckley.

The Leeds boss was in his second full season at Elland Road and still rebuilding the squad following the club's relegation to the Second Division in 1946/47. Kerfoot made his senior debut against QPR within days of joining; however, it wasn't until the start of the 1950/51 season that he established himself in the side.

For the second year running Leeds had ended a league campaign in fifth place, which was frustrating because there were some fine players at the club. Slipping to sixth in 1951/52, Kerfoot grabbed his first goal for the club in a 3-1 against Notts County.

When Leeds finished tenth in 1952/53, Raich Carter took over as manager. Not renowned for his goalscoring, bizarrely Kerfoot scored in the last two games of the season when Leeds defeated Nottingham Forest 2-1 and drew with Doncaster Rovers 1-1. Another top-ten finish saw Kerfoot promoted to captain for the 1954/55 season. Recovering from four defeats in the opening five fixtures, Leeds missed promotion by just one point and Kerfoot scored his only FA Cup goal in a 2-2 draw against Torquay United. Leeds lost the replay.

Another change at skipper saw John Charles lead the team out in 1955/56. However, Leeds stuttered during the early stages until Carter switched his captain to centre forward. The team improved but it wasn't until late on that they made a significant challenge, winning eight of their last nine games to secure promotion as runners-up behind Sheffield Wednesday. Kerfoot had been consistent throughout the campaign and for the second time was an ever-present in the team.

Kerfoot would not miss another game for two seasons. Finishing eighth was a tremendous effort, but following Charles' departure to Juventus in 1957, Leeds struggled for goals and Kerfoot's last couple of years at the club saw the team battling at the wrong end of the table. At the end of the 1958/59 campaign Kerfoot joined Chesterfield, but retired in 1960 after just 9 appearances.

Eric Kerfoot, who died in 1980, played 349 games for Leeds United, scoring 10 goals. An ever-present on four occasions, he missed thirteen games in eight seasons, and between 1953/54 and 1957/58 was absent on only five occasions. Although not the tallest of players, Kerfoot was loyal, enthusiastic, intelligent and had great distribution skills. Always encouraging and a team player, Kerfoot drove the team forward at every opportunity.

Harry Kewell made an extraordinary start to his Leeds United career. A product of New South Wales' school academy in Australia, Kewell began the 1995/96 season in the club's youth team. By the end, the talented Aussie had played for the reserves, first team and his country! The next few seasons would see Kewell become one of the most exciting prospects in the game.

Born in Sydney on 22 September 1978, Kewell was the pick of many talented youngsters at the club and under the watchful eye of Eddie Gray developed into a sensational prospect. The star of the team that won the FA Youth Cup in 1997, after his first team debut against Middlesborough in March 1996, George Graham unleashed Kewell on the Premier League during the 1997/98 season. A lot was expected from the youngster and he didn't disappoint.

Playing on the left side of midfield or in attack alongside Jimmy Floyd Hasselbaink, Kewell gave opposing defences the runaround and it was clear he was a future star. During an entertaining campaign when Leeds qualified for Europe, Kewell scored 8 goals, including a terrific strike in a classic match when Leeds came from three goals down to defeat Derby County 4-3.

Kewell got off to a slow start in 1998/99, but following David O'Leary's appointment as manager, the season was reignited with the introduction of a number of Kewell's contemporaries from the youth team. A seven-game winning sequence in the second half of the season, that included Kewell strikes at Leicester City and against Tottenham Hotspur, all but clinched a UEFA Cup spot.

The 1999/2000 campaign would see Kewell's best season for Leeds, striking 16 goals as Leeds qualified for the Champions League and reached the semi-finals of the UEFA Cup. Among many classy moments were a terrific strike against Roma and an outrageous chip against Sheffield Wednesday, but his most remarkable goal came against Aston Villa. Cutting in from the left flank, Kewell's ferocious thirty-five-yard drive was unbelievable. Kewell won Leeds United's Player of the Year and the PFA Young Player of the Year awards.

Unfortunately, injuries began to hamper Kewell, although he did play his part in Leeds' remarkable run to the Champions League semi-finals. His country's failure to make the 2002 World Cup finals was a major disappointment, but he is determined to represent Australia at the game's premier tournament.

Inconsistency, a tendency to drift out of a game for long phases and persistent rumours of a move in 2002/03 made supporters wonder about Kewell's commitment to club, but his ability to destroy any defence remained. Powerful in the air, quick off the mark and blessed with sublime skills, sensational solo efforts against Grasshoppers of Zurich in the UEFA Cup, Crystal Palace in the FA Cup and Arsenal in the Premiership demonstrated his abilities.

However, after helping Leeds avoid relegation, the circumstances and terms surrounding his £5m departure to Liverpool during the close season angered Leeds followers. As the club contemplates life in Division One, memories of Kewell's prodigious talent and his 63 goals in 254 (+10 substitute) matches, are now just a distant memory. Nevertheless, during eight years at Leeds United the Wizard of Oz provided exceptional flashes of inspiration.

PETER LORIMER ————————————

Peter Lorimer is the most prolific goalscorer in Leeds United's history. Records are made to be broken but his tally of 238 goals in all competitions, 81 more than the legendary John Charles, is surely beyond anyone.

Born in Dundee on 11 December 1946, Lorimer was a prodigious schoolboy talent, scoring 176 goals in one season! With numerous clubs chasing his signature, Don Revie worked tirelessly to add him to join his crop of youngsters at Elland Road. His efforts would be richly rewarded.

Joining Leeds in May 1962, Lorimer became the club's youngest debutant when he faced Southampton aged 15 years 289 days, but he didn't become a regular until the 1965/66 campaign. Opening his account in a 3-2 defeat at Tottenham Hotspur, Lorimer scored a brace in victories against Blackburn Rovers, Northampton Town and Nottingham Forest. He also grabbed his first hat-trick in an FA Cup tie against Bury and finished top scorer on 19 goals.

Leading scorer two years later with 30 goals, his highest total for Leeds, the 1967/68 campaign saw Leeds win the League Cup and Fairs Cup. Lorimer was leading scorer in both competitions and among his European goals, four came against Spora Luxembourg in a club-record 9-0 win, and his strikes against Partizan Belgrade and Rangers proved crucial. In the league, Lorimer won clashes against Burnley, West Ham and Tottenham, and scored in Leeds' 7-0 win against Chelsea.

Leeds were at the height of their powers and after winning the First Division title in 1968/69, only fixture congestion denied them more trophies the following term when they finished runners-up in all three major competitions. It was a bitter disappointment, but honours arrived in 1970/71 with the Fairs Cup. Lorimer top scored with five goals, including vital strikes against Dynamo Dresden and Vitoria Setubal.

In 1971/72, Lorimer completed his domestic collection with an FA Cup winners' medal. The club's Player of the Year, his haul of 29 goals included a hat-trick in Leeds' 7-0

Lorimer scores for Leeds against Nottingham Forest.

demolition of Southampton. The following campaign would be notable for Leeds missing out in both the FA Cup and European Cup Winners' Cup finals, but the lasting memory was Jim Montgomery's outrageous save from Lorimer at Wembley. Three decades on the Sunderland 'keeper's point-blank save still defies belief.

Twelve months on Leeds claimed another First Division crown, but made hard work of it after beginning the 1973/74 campaign with a twenty-nine-game unbeaten run. Although not his most prolific season, Lorimer grabbed a hat-trick against Birmingham City but his four goals in the run-in proved more crucial as Leeds came through a sticky spell. The relief following his strikes in 2-0 victories against Derby County and Sheffield United and his goal in the

Lorimer crashes home against Huddersfield Town.

3-2 win over Ipswich Town was extraordinary. The latter result ultimately clinched the title.

Following Don Revie's departure during the close season, Jimmy Armfield eventually took the helm and during a memorable European Cup campaign, Lorimer scored arguably his most crucial goal for Leeds against Barcelona to clinch a place in the final. His brilliant volley against Bayern Munich looked to have won the trophy but was ruled out because Billy Bremner had strayed offside. Alongside his last-minute free-kick against Chelsea in the 1967 FA Cup semi-final, both efforts are still the most debated disallowed goals in the club's history.

As former colleagues moved on, Leeds were no longer title contenders but were unlucky not to win silverware, falling at the semi-final stages of the FA Cup in 1977 and League Cup in 1978. After sixteen seasons at the club, Lorimer embarked on a five-year spell at Toronto Blizzards, Vancouver Whitecaps and York City before returning to Leeds in December 1983 following a request by ex-teammate Eddie Gray to help his former club, who were languishing near the bottom of the Second Division.

Playing in midfield, Lorimer helped Leeds finish tenth and on a historical note finally overhauled John Charles' record of 153 league goals with a penalty against Oldham Athletic. Lorimer played his final game for Leeds against Grimsby Town in 1985 at the age of thirty-nine. Following a brief spell at Whitby and Hapoel Haifa, Lorimer retired after twenty-four seasons as a professional footballer.

Dubbed 'Hotshot' Lorimer, 'keepers domestically and in Europe grasped air on numerous occasions. When it came to free-kicks, Lorimer's prowess was legendary and he scored countless goals down the years. Dangerous from anywhere in an opponents' half; Lorimer

PETER LORIMER

Lorimer in action in the European Cup Winners Cup.

once scored from the halfway line! His power made him a natural penalty expert, but he had to wait at Leeds because Johnny Giles was the undisputed number one. Nevertheless, after scoring his first spot kick against Preston North End in 1966, Lorimer scored thirty-two penalties, second only to Giles.

This remarkable player was not just a goalscorer though. Lorimer could spread play with superb accuracy, created many goals for Allan Clarke and Mick Jones with pinpoint crosses from the right flank, and blessed with poise and ball control, could take on the best full-backs around.

On the international stage, Lorimer represented Scotland as an amateur prior to making his full Scottish debut in 1969 against Spain. Bizarrely, this clash came a month before his Under-23 debut against France! Following one more appearance for the Under-23s, Lorimer gained 21 caps for his country, scoring 4 goals. Among a number of memorable performances, Lorimer played in the 1974 World Cup finals, scoring a trademark volley against Zaire.

In recent years, Lorimer has become an accomplished radio summariser and returned to the club as a director in 2004. Extremely popular with supporters, Peter Lorimer is one of the club's greatest ever players. Sixth on the all-time list with 677 (+28 substitute) appearances, but for his spell away from the club he would have claimed this record on top of his goalscoring achievements. One of only four players alongside Tom Jennings, John Charles and Lee Chapman to score thirty goals in a season, for supporters the lasting memory of Peter Lorimer will be of him unleashing a thunderbolt during his heyday. There was no finer sight.

John Lukic is one of the few players in Leeds United's history to have played across three
decades (1970s-1990s). Breaking into the team in 1979, Lukic served the club through a
difficult era during the club's slide into the Second Division before returning in 1990 as Leeds
established themselves as a major force in the game. Lukic is one of only two players, Gary
Kelly being the other, to make 400 appearances for the club since the Don Revie era.

Born in Chesterfield on 11 December 1960, Leeds scouts spotted Lukic playing in
Derbyshire schools football prior to joining the club in 1978. Initially the teenager replaced
veteran 'keeper David Harvey and held off the challenge of David Seaman, an apprentice at

the time. After a League debut against Brighton in 1979, Lukic proceeded to play a club record 146 successive games.

Lukic had a bright future ahead of him and in September 1980 won the first of 7 Under-21 caps for England, but the club's relegation to the Second Division forced him to consider his long-term future. A rising star in the game, Lukic was dropped after his transfer request and a £125,000 transfer fee took him to Arsenal, where over seven seasons he gained League Championship and League Cup winners' medals.

During the 1989/90 close season Lukic needed a new club after the arrival of Seaman at Arsenal. Coming full circle, Howard Wilkinson made Lukic Leeds' first £1m goalkeeper following Leeds' return to the First Division. Back at Elland Road, Lukic slotted in as if he had never been away. From the opening game of the 1990/91 season Lukic was sensational. A 'keeper of the highest calibre, Lukic was commanding in the air, brave, a terrific shot-stopper, and possessed brilliant reflexes. His performances gained him selection to the England 'B' squad.

Although somewhat surprisingly a full cap never materialised, Lukic did add another medal to his collection as Leeds overhauled Manchester United to win the 1991/92 First Division Championship. An ever-present throughout the campaign, Lukic kept nineteen clean sheets and during the run-in conceded only two goals as Leeds won four of their five remaining games to clinch the title.

After helping Leeds to a Charity Shield triumph over Liverpool, Lukic's confidence dipped during the 1992/93 season. His gaffe against Rangers in the European Cup didn't help matters, and after losing his place to Mark Beeney, he returned in 1994/95 as Leeds snatched a European spot with a sensational run that saw them win six of their last eight games.

In 1996, Lukic helped Leeds reach a first Wembley cup final in twenty-three years, before returning to his former club on a free transfer as Seaman's understudy with the impending arrival at Elland Road of Nigel Martyn. A member of the squad that won the double in 1997/98, Lukic finally retired at the end of the 1999/2000 season.

One of Leeds United's most consistent and tallest goalkeepers, John Lukic made 413 appearances for Leeds during two spells at the club. Player of the Year in his first spell at the club in 1979/80, Lukic will be best remembered for his form during the 1991/92 title campaign when he was one of the principal reasons for Leeds' success that term.

G ary McAllister arrived at Leeds United for £1m following the club's promotion to the First Division in 1990. The Scot was no stranger to Leeds' supporters; indeed his performance for Leicester City in the penultimate game of the 1989/90 season nearly cost his future teammates promotion. Although Leeds won the match, McAllister scored a terrific goal and nearly stole victory, before Gordon Strachan's late winner. McAllister would prove a marvellous acquisition.

Born in Motherwell on 25 December 1964, McAllister joined his hometown club in 1981 before moving to Leicester four years later where he enhanced his reputation. Having won 3 caps for Scotland, McAllister was in demand. Out of contract, Nottingham Forest attempted to sign him but the Scot turned down Brian Clough's overtures in favour of Howard Wilkinson's ambitious plans at Leeds.

Replacing cult hero Vinnie Jones in midfield, McAllister made his debut at the start of the 1990/91 season against Everton. Adding balance to the left side of midfield and a touch of panache alongside Strachan, David Batty and Gary Speed, McAllister played his part as Leeds surprised many pundits by reaching the semi-finals of the League Cup and finishing a memorable First Division campaign in the top-four.

McAllister scored in the opening fixture in 1991/92 against Nottingham Forest with a crisp strike and went on to play a pivotal role in the club's success that term. During the campaign, he scored five goals, including a sensational strike at Notts County, but none more important than a crucial penalty in a 2-0 win over Coventry City during the run-in. A few days later in the penultimate game, his pinpoint cross for Jon Newsome's header at Sheffield United proved vital in a 3-2 win. Within hours, Leeds had been crowned champions.

GARY McALLISTER

Manchester United's Steve Bruce (left) challenges Leeds United's Gary McAllister.

A cultured midfield player with exceptional positional sense, McAllister skippered Leeds to a thrilling 4-3 win over Liverpool at Wembley in the Charity Shield. The club's Player of the Year in 1993/94, McAllister took over as captain the following season and revelled in the extra responsibility.

With Strachan moving on, McAllister was the driving force from central midfield. Picking out his strikers with pinpoint passes, he was adept at surging forward to strike at goal. Sensational throughout the campaign, Leeds snatched a UEFA Cup place with a tremendous run-in. In 1995/96 McAllister scored a brilliant hat-trick against Coventry City. Leeds marched to the League Cup final and quarter-finals of the FA Cup, however a disastrous few days saw them lose at Wembley and crash out of the premier domestic cup competition.

Throughout his spell at Leeds, McAllister was a regular in the Scotland XI. Winning 58 caps, he led his country in the Euro '96 finals. Although he performed well, a penalty miss against England proved crucial in Scotland's elimination from the competition.

McAllister's £3m transfer to Coventry upset Leeds supporters who made their feelings known on his return visits. After four seasons battling against relegation, McAllister clinched a move to Liverpool, where his performances proved instrumental in their treble-cup winning season in 2000/01.

Gary McAllister enjoyed an outstanding career. Scoring 45 goals in his 294 (+1 substitute) appearances for Leeds, McAllister was a superb passer of the ball and like all great midfielders was able to find space out of nowhere. An expert at dead-ball situations, McAllister was arguably the best distributor of a ball since the days of Johnny Giles.

Duncan McKenzie was a born headline-maker and Leeds United supporters loved his unique skills and antics whether nonchalantly scoring a goal, setting up a colleague with an outrageous flick, jumping over a mini or throwing a golf ball the length of a football pitch. Whenever McKenzie played, you were always guaranteed entertainment, even if his teammates and opposing defenders were unsure sometimes what he'd do next!

Born 10 June 1950, McKenzie began his career at Nottingham Forest in July 1968. Following a couple of loan spells at Mansfield, McKenzie established himself in the side. When Brian Clough arrived at Leeds, he promptly paid Forest £240,000 in August 1974 for his services and gave him his debut against Liverpool at Wembley in the Charity Shield. It would be a while before Clough's successor, Jimmy Armfield, gave McKenzie an extended opportunity to impress.

When Allan Clarke missed a clash against Arsenal a couple of months into the 1975/76 season, McKenzie played and scored both goals in a sensational performance. On Clarke's return, McKenzie was dropped but he was soon back and stayed in the side. A brace against Middlesbrough sparked a blitz of 9 goals in 12 games. Flamboyant and creative, fans loved his unpredictability. By the end of the season, he had finished second-top scorer behind Clarke.

In a difficult campaign Leeds reached the quarter-finals of the FA Cup before going out to Ipswich Town after three replays, McKenzie scoring a last-minute equaliser in the second encounter. However, he hardly featured in the European Cup campaign after his dismissal against Ujpest Dozsa in the second round.

During his second season at Leeds, with Joe Jordan and Peter Lorimer out for long spells, McKenzie again teamed up with Clarke in attack. After a slow opening, McKenzie again sparked a great run with 11 goals in as many games, including a brilliant two-goal display against Leicester City in front of Elland Road's biggest gate of the season just after Christmas. The run raised hopes of a title challenge briefly, but inconsistency saw Leeds end the campaign in fifth place.

McKenzie was incredibly popular with supporters, far more than Clough's other signings, and many were saddened when he joined Anderlecht at the end of the season for £200,000. Within six months, another £200,000 transfer took him to Everton, where he played in the 1977 League Cup final. Thereafter his travels included spells at Chelsea, Blackburn Rovers and Tulsa Roughnecks in the American NASL.

An accomplished after-dinner speaker, in a career that had many twists and turns, Leeds supporters enjoyed his brief spell, in which he scored 30 goals in 76 (+6 substitute) appearances. Many players have played more games for the club, but created far fewer memories. Duncan McKenzie left his unique mark at Leeds United.

McKenzie fires home for Leeds against Norwich.

123

Billy McLeod was the first goalscoring hero for football followers in the city of Leeds. Undoubtedly the star of the team, McLeod played more games and scored more goals than anyone in Leeds City's fifteen-year history.

Born in County Durham, June 1887, McLeod played his early football at Hebburn Argyle, Peebles Rovers and Lincoln City prior to a £350 transfer to City in November 1906. Following his debut the same month against Wolves, McLeod scored the winning goal in a 3-2 win against Clapton Orient in the next match, and ended his first season as top scorer with 16 goals from 24 league and FA Cup appearances.

City's tenth-place finish would not be bettered for five seasons, which resulted in Herbert Chapman succeeding Frank Scott-Walford as manager at the end of the 1911/12 campaign. With McLeod being top scorer in each of his seasons at the club, Chapman realised that to improve the team's prospects he had to supply more opportunities for his star striker who had twice struck 17 goals in a campaign.

Revamping his forward line with the introduction of new signings during the 1912/13 season had the desired effect. Scoring a club-record seventy goals, City finished sixth for the first time since their inaugural campaign. As for McLeod, his 27 league goals were a club record by some distance. Notching 12 in 9 games, he grabbed his first hat-tricks for the club against Glossop and Bury.

A similar story unfolded in 1913/14. McLeod again scored 27 league goals, including trebles against Wolves and Huddersfield, and four against Nottingham Forest in an 8-0 win; a record score for a league match. Finishing fourth, City missed promotion by two points. It would prove to be City's highest Second Division finish before the First World War, although in the final campaign before the war, when City finished fifteenth, McLeod became the only City player to score five goals in a match in a 6-2 victory at Hull City. In a century of football in the city, Gordon Hodgson of Leeds United in 1937/38 is the only professional footballer to match McLeod's five-goal performance.

During the hostilities, McLeod played for Bradford City while working for an engineering firm and made 13 appearances for Leeds, scoring 6 goals. McLeod scored a brace in the opening Second Division fixture against Blackpool in 1919/20; however his hat-trick against Wolves on 4 October 1919 would be his final goals for the club due to the illegal payments scandal that saw Leeds City expelled from the Football League.

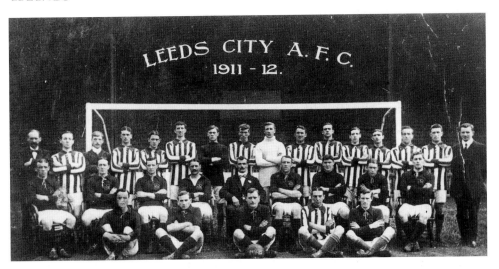

Leeds City FC – 1911/12 season. Back row: S.Collins (Trainer), J. Clarkin, A. Stead, S. Johnson, G. Cunningham, J. Heaney, A. Hogg, E. McDaniel, L. Murphy, J. Moran, A. Roberts, R. Roberts, W. Briggs, M. Foley, J. Fortune, H. Harbourne. Middle row: H.P. Roberts, T. Mulholland, J. Harkins, S. Cubberley, F. Scott Walford, T. Morris, C. Kelly, J. Enright, F. Croot. Bottom row: A. Creichton, G. Affleck, W. McLeod, W. Gillespie, H. Bridgett.

S. Whittham & Sons auctioned the players at the Metropole Hotel with McLeod generating the greatest fee of £1,250 from Notts County. After two years, he played briefly for Doncaster Rovers. Although a prolific scorer, the closest McLeod came to representing England was as a non-playing reserve against Wales in 1914, the same year he sat on the bench for the Football League in a representative match against the Scottish League.

When analysing the history of Leeds City, the name of Billy McLeod will never be forgotten. The only City player to score five goals in a game and make over 300 appearances, McLeod was top scorer in nine consecutive seasons, he was also leading the scoring chart at the time of City's demise. Fred Croot with 38 goals is City's second-top goalscorer, which makes McLeod's final tally of 177 goals in 301 matches all the more remarkable and says everything about this amazing footballer.

Gordon McQueen took on the mantle of following in the footsteps of Jack Charlton and quickly succeeded, despite his tender years, in becoming a linchpin of defence during the mid-1970s.

Born in Kilbirnie on 26 June 1952, McQueen could have been a goalkeeper like his father, who played for Hibernian, Berwick Rangers and East Fife, or a winger, but matured into a centre half despite his failure to impress in trials at Liverpool and Rangers. Undaunted, McQueen persevered and joined St Mirren in 1970.

For some time Don Revie had been looking for a long-term replacement for Jack Charlton. Revie had experimented with John Faulkner and Roy Ellam, but neither made the transition to the first XI whereas Revie spotted raw potential in McQueen, and after a £30,000 move in September 1972, the Scot rapidly progressed. Impressing on his debut at Derby County in a hard-fought 3–2 win, McQueen ended the season by playing against AC Milan in the European Cup Winners' Cup final.

By the start of the 1973/74, with Big Jack finally retiring, McQueen started in the first team and immediately developed an understanding with Norman Hunter in central defence. As Leeds created a club-record twenty-nine-game unbeaten run, McQueen grew in stature and played his part as Leeds clinched the First Division title. At the end of the season, he won his first Scotland cap and made the provisional squad for the 1974 World Cup finals in Germany.

Following Revie's departure, McQueen played in the Charity Shield against Liverpool at Wembley and matured throughout a difficult campaign in 1974/75 that culminated in the European Cup final defeat to Bayern Munich. Unluckily, McQueen, who scored vital goals against Anderlecht and Ujpesti Dosza, missed the final following his sending-off against Barcelona in the semi-final.

Bar a spell out with an Achilles tendon injury in 1975/76, over the next three seasons McQueen held the defence together alongside Hunter, Paul Madeley and Trevor Cherry as a revamped Leeds side came close to honours during a difficult transitional period. A towering centre half, McQueen dominated opponents with his sheer presence. Comfortable on the ball, exceptional in the air, a solid tackler and determined, McQueen was a formidable opponent. A majestic sight in full flow, McQueen loved breaking from defence to start an attack.

The popular Scot also caused havoc at set pieces, especially in 1976/77 when he finished the season second-top scorer with eight goals, notching winners against West Brom, Birmingham City and a late two-goal burst to snatch a victory against Middlesbrough, which sent Elland Road into raptures.

A regular for Scotland, his most memorable moment was at Wembley in the 1977 Home Internationals when he scored in a famous 2–1 win, a match made notable when the Tartan Army destroyed the goalposts during their celebrations at the end. Sadly, he missed both the 1978 and 1982 World Cup finals through injuries, which would have capped an international career that saw him win 30 caps for his country.

McQueen enraged Leeds supporters when he followed Joe Jordan to Manchester United for a British-record fee of £495,000 in 1978. Injuries restricted his appearances; however, McQueen scored in the 1979 FA Cup final against Arsenal and collected a winners' medal in

1983. At the end of 1984/85 McQueen joined Seiko FC (Hong Kong) as player–coach prior to managing Airdrie, coaching St Mirren and teaming up with Bryan Robson at Middlesbrough as reserve-team coach in 1994, a position he held until the end of the 2000/01 season.

Gordon McQueen scored 19 goals in 171 (+1 substitute) appearances for Leeds United. Player of the Year twice in 1974/75 and 1976/77, McQueen did a superb job at Elland Road in the mid-1970s.

Paul Madeley joined Leeds United as an apprentice in 1961 and went on to become the most versatile player in the club's history during a seventeen-year career. Indeed, after making his debut against Manchester City in January 1964, as a replacement for Jack Charlton, such was his ability to play in different positions that he was not regarded as simply a full-back, centre half or midfielder because he could play anywhere; and did.

Born in Leeds on 20 September 1944, Madeley had two nicknames: 'Mr Versatile', due to his flexibility, and 'Rolls Royce', because of the smooth manner in which he glided around a football field. Remarkably, Madeley appeared in every outfield position. Indeed, in 1966/67, Madeley wore every shirt bar number eleven!

One of the fittest players in the squad, despite not having a dedicated role in Revie's legendary team, Madeley was always in the starting XI whether due to an injury, suspension or tactical reasoning. This ability was vital to Leeds' success during the Revie era because he was able to slot into different positions at a moment's notice without affecting the balance of the side.

Analysing the roles Madeley played for Leeds, especially in cup finals, it is easy to understand why this remarkable player was so important to the team. Madeley holds the unique achievement for Leeds of playing in four domestic cup finals at Wembley in four different positions: 1968 League Cup (centre forward); 1970 FA Cup (right-back), 1972 FA Cup (left-back) and 1973 FA Cup (centre half). In addition, Madeley played on the left side of midfield in the 1968 and 1971 Fairs Cup finals and the 1973 European Cup Winners' Cup final, and centre half in the 1975 European Cup final.

Not renowned as a goalscorer, Madeley scored the first of 34 goals for Leeds with a long-range strike at Leicester City in September 1965, before enjoying his most prolific season in 1967/68. Playing as an auxiliary striker for a period, apart from several others, Madeley notched 10 goals in all competitions. Scoring a brace against Southampton in a 5-0 win, Madeley struck in a club-record 9-0 win against Spora Luxembourg and his header earned Leeds a 1-1 draw at Dundee during a Fairs Cup semi-final clash, Leeds winning the tie 2-1 on aggregate.

Three years on, colleagues dubbed him 'goal-a-game' Madeley after strikes against Blackpool, Stoke City and Wolves in consecutive games! However, the most important goal of his illustrious career came at the end of the 1970/71 campaign against Juventus in the first leg of the Fairs Cup final when Leeds won the trophy on away goals. Thereafter, goals were very much at a premium, Madeley's seventh in eight seasons securing a 4-0 win against Southampton in November 1978.

In an outstanding career, Madeley helped Leeds win the First Division Championship and Fairs Cup twice, the FA Cup, League Cup and Charity Shield. He also featured in European Cup Winners' Cup, European Cup and two FA Cup finals, and finished as a First Division runner-up on no fewer than five occasions.

Following Don Revie's departure and the European Cup final defeat to Bayern Munich in 1974/75, as numerous colleagues moved on, Madeley played alongside Gordon McQueen and Paul Hart in central defence. Serving a number of managers in the late 1970s, although not title contenders, Leeds finished fifth in 1975/76 and 1978/79 and reached FA Cup and League Cup semi-finals.

Madeley heads home against Blackpool.

On the international stage, Madeley hit the headlines when he dropped out of Sir Alf Ramsey's twenty-eight-man squad that was due to travel to the 1970 World Cup finals. Ramsey, however, understood Madeley's reasons and gave him his full debut against Northern Ireland in 1971. As with Leeds, Madeley represented his country in a variety of positions in defence or midfield, winning a total of 24 caps.

The club's Player of the Year in 1975/76, Madeley was world class in a number of positions. A ball-winner and playmaker, Madeley had great positional awareness, natural strength and was superb in the air. Of all the roles he filled, playing the defensive midfield role demonstrated his abilities best. His long stride enabled him to make ground quickly before playing a sweeping pass or deft flicks, and his tackles were crisp and immaculately timed.

Retiring in 1980, he joined the family's successful chain of home decor stores. Fifth on the all-time list following his 712 (+14 substitute) appearances for the club, Madeley played a club record 50 League Cup ties. A one-club player, Paul Madeley was priceless for Leeds United.

NIGEL MARTYN

Nigel Martyn was the ultimate professional during his years at Leeds United. Immensely popular with supporters, Martyn's prowess made him one of British football's top goalkeepers during the last decade.

Born in St Austell on 11 August 1966, Martyn began his career in 1987 at Bristol Rovers, before a move to Crystal Palace two years later made him the first £1m goalkeeper. In seven eventful seasons, Martyn experienced promotion, relegation and played in the 1990 FA Cup final. After more than 300 appearances for the Eagles, where he gained his first England cap in 1992, Howard Wilkinson persuaded Martyn to join Leeds in July 1996 for £2.25m, another British record.

Following his debut against Derby County on the opening day of the 1996/97 season, Martyn's early experiences at Elland Road could not have been more awkward with the departure of Wilkinson after five league fixtures, but he coped brilliantly and won rave reviews as Leeds finished mid-table. Keeping twenty-two clean sheets, Martyn was voted the club's Player of the Year and helped Leeds qualify for the UEFA Cup the following term with some exceptional displays.

A member of England's 1998 World Cup squad, Martyn's composure was vital during the early stages of the 1998/99 season when David O'Leary succeeded George Graham as manager, and immediately blooded a number of youngsters. O'Leary's bold policy worked and the campaign took off with a number of thrilling victories before a seven-game winning sequence went a long way to clinching a UEFA Cup spot again.

Leeds had a superb mix of youth and experience and during a memorable 1999/00 campaign, which saw Martyn recognised in the Premier League's Team of the Year, Leeds qualified for the Champions League and reached the semi-finals of the UEFA Cup. At Euro 2000, Martyn played against Romania in the final qualifying game when David Seaman picked up an injury. Although he made some great saves, a combination of poor defending and one goalkeeping error resulted in an early exit from the competition. A member of the 2002 World Cup squad, Martyn won 23 caps for England.

In 2000/01 Martyn had his first lengthy absence through injury and had to battle to win his place back in the side following Paul Robinson's form as deputy. On his return Martyn showed his true class as Leeds capped a tremendous season by reaching the semi-finals of the Champions League. Although Leeds qualified for Europe in 2001/02, the following term Martyn was demoted to the bench as Leeds just avoided relegation.

With Robinson regarded as Leeds' number-one 'keeper it was no surprise when Martyn moved to Everton during the 2003/04 campaign. Reliable as ever, Martyn enjoyed an outstanding season, and his performances, notably on his first return to Elland Road when he single-handedly kept his side in the game during the run-in, saved his new club from relegation.

During seven years at Elland Road, Nigel Martyn gave outstanding service. Commanding in the air, a sensational shot-stopper and possessing supreme reflexes, his consistent form was one of the major factors in Leeds' resurgence as a major force under O'Leary. Nigel Martyn made 273 appearances for Leeds United and ranks as one of the club's greatest ever goalkeepers.

Bill Menzies was one of Leeds United's most loyal players during the club's formative years. A steadfast member of the side, over a twelve-year period Menzies experienced promotion and relegation twice, and played with many of the great stars of the era.

Born in Bucksburn near Aberdeen on 10 July 1901, Arthur Fairclough persuaded Menzies to join the club from Mungiemoss in 1922 but he would not make his debut against Oldham Athletic until Boxing Day 1923. Following Leeds' 5-0 win, Menzies kept his place as Leeds stayed in the hunt for the Second Division Championship, which was duly claimed in the penultimate game when Leeds defeated Nelson.

Throughout much of their initial stay in the top flight, Menzies played alongside stalwarts Bert Duffield, Willis Edwards and Ernie Hart, but Leeds struggled and suffered relegation in 1926/27. The campaign saw the resolute left-back score his only league goal for Leeds in a 3-2 defeat at West Ham.

Back in the Second Division, with Dick Ray at the helm, Leeds began the new campaign well. Two unbeaten runs underpinned the promotion drive, the latter a club record when the players conceded no goals in nine games. A defeat in the last home game cost the title but Leeds had regained their First Division status.

After a season of consolidation, when Menzies notched his second and final goal for Leeds during a 2-2 draw at Exeter City in the FA Cup, Ray's team surprised opponents when they finished fifth in 1929/30, their highest placing since formation. Leeds were one of the favourites to challenge for the title, but although Jack Milburn and Wilf Copping strengthened the defence, the new campaign was a disaster.

On occasion Leeds annihilated the opposition, as Middlesbrough (7-0) and Manchester United (5-0) experienced, but the majority of the campaign saw inconsistent spells. Relegation came on the last day of the season. Once again, the players showed tremendous resolve by bouncing back at the first attempt.

Leeds challenged for the title but eventually settled for the runners-up spot. For Menzies, who played the majority of the 1931/32 campaign, the final match of the season against Port Vale would be his last due to injury. In September 1933, Menzies played for Goole Town briefly before embarking on a coaching career with the West Riding FA.

Bill Menzies is standing, third from left, 1924-25.

Unlucky never to win a full cap for Scotland, Menzies was quick, intelligent and his positional awareness made life difficult for opposing wingers. For six seasons, he was unchallenged in his position, making 258 appearances.

Battling away as the club established themselves as a professional club, Bill Menzies, who died in 1970, was a tremendous servant to Leeds United, and alongside Hart is the only Leeds player to play in the Second Division Championship side and both promotion campaigns of the pre-war era.

GEORGE MILBURN

George Milburn was one of three brothers to represent Leeds United throughout a twenty-four-year period. At one point during the late 1930s, George, Jack and Jim were on the playing staff at the club, but didn't play in a first XI game together.

The Milburn family over five decades placed Ashington on the football map. A fourth brother, Stan, played for

Milburn stands fourth from right, 1929-30.

Leicester City, Rochdale and Chesterfield. Cousin Jackie Milburn was a legend at Newcastle United while nephews Jack and Bobby Charlton became World Cup heroes with England.

Born in Ashington on 24 June 1910, George was the second oldest of the Milburn trio and quickly attracted the attention of clubs as a promising centre-back for his hometown club. Spotted by Leeds scouts, manager Dick Ray brought the teenager to Elland Road in March 1928 and converted him to right-back.

George made his debut at Sheffield Wednesday in November 1928, but would play mainly in the reserves due to the excellent form of brother Jack, twenty-one months his senior, and Bill Menzies. Patience was the key and George finally received an extended run during the 1930/31 season when Menzies was injured.

Leeds had just finished the previous First Division campaign in fifth place, so there was genuine belief that the team could challenge for the title. However, despite great wins against Blackpool 7-3 and Manchester United 5-0 the majority of the campaign was a relegation battle, which was finally lost on the last day of the season.

The following term George was in and out of the side as Leeds regained top-flight status. However, due to a long-term injury to Menzies, George received his opportunity to partner Jack in defence on a regular basis from the start of the 1932/33 season. Leeds finished eighth and the brothers appeared in every league game. In 1933/34 Leeds finished the season ninth, the highlight being a club record 8-0 win against Leicester City.

The emergence of Bert Sprotson ended George's automatic place in the first XI. Making sporadic first-team appearances for three seasons, George captained the reserves to the club's first Central League title in 1936/37, a feat unequalled for sixty years, but with limited opportunities George agreed to join Chesterfield in May 1937.

A guest player for Leeds and Yeovil Town during the war, George teamed up with Stan after the hostilites at Chesterfield, and became one of the few players to score a hat-trick of penalties in a match, against Sheffield Wednesday on 7 June 1947, before taking on the role of assistant manager.

George Milburn, who died in 1980, made 166 appearances for Leeds United, scoring just once, against Portsmouth in 1935. Partnering elder brother Jack on 153 occasions for Leeds, George was loyal, reliable and totally committed to Leeds United.

Jack Milburn joined Leeds United from Spen Black & White in November 1928. The eldest of three brothers to represent the club, all full-backs, Jack enjoyed the greatest success, making 408 appearances during the 1930s.

Part of the legendary Milburn family, cousin Jackie Milburn was a Newcastle United legend, whilst nephews Jack and Bobby Charlton helped England win the 1966 World Cup. Although Jack, George and Jim were at Leeds at one stage, they didn't play a first-team game together.

Born in Ashington on 18 March 1908, Jack made his First Division debut against Everton in September 1929. His elevation from a season in the reserves was fortuitous, because his appearance coincided with the first of seven successive wins and Dick Ray was unwilling to change a winning side. Leeds went on to finish fifth and recorded a club-record 8-1 win in the FA Cup against Crystal Palace.

There was genuine belief that Leeds could challenge for the title in 1930/31, but astonishingly the majority of the campaign was a relegation battle, which was lost on the last day of the season. During the 1931/32 campaign, Ray's players were determined to bounce back. Two wins in the last ten games cost the title but the runners-up spot was rarely in doubt. The only ever-present in the side, Jack had developed a fearsome reputation for his tackling and a thunderous shot earned him the responsibility of taking penalties, scoring against QPR and Nottingham Forest.

Leeds United 1944-5. Back row: Roxburgh (Trainer), Butterworth, Shotton, Twomey, Jack Milburn, Campbell, Weaver. Front row: Burbanks, Coyne, Henry, Hindle, Paton.

At the start of the 1932/33 campaign, Jack succeeded Bill Menzies at left-back, enabling brother George to play right-back. They would partner each other on 153 occasions. For two seasons, Leeds consolidated their position in the top-ten, the highlight a club-record 8-0 win over Leicester City in April 1934. However, 1934/35 would be anything but comfortable. With relegation looming, Billy Hampson replaced Ray as manager. It was tight, but Leeds avoided relegation.

Throughout his Leeds career, Jack was a supreme penalty taker. During the 1935/36 season, he created a club record when he despatched nine, including three in consecutive league games against Huddersfield, West Brom and Middlesbrough, the first player to achieve such a feat. The third most prolific penalty taker for Leeds behind Johnny Giles, who matched Jack's feat of converting penalties in three successive league games in 1972/73, and Peter Lorimer, of George's 30 goals for the club, 29 were penalties!

The 1936/37 campaign brought another relegation scrap. In a tense finale, Jack scored crucial penalties against Sunderland and Portsmouth in the final two games, both at Elland Road, to help secure safety. His latter years would see Leeds sit comfortably in mid-table, the highlight an 8-2 win over Leicester City, a result not bettered until 1967.

With first-team opportunities limited, Jack joined Norwich City towards the end of the 1938/39 season. Returning to play 64 wartime games for Leeds, when league football resumed, he enjoyed a brief spell at Bradford City, later managing them, before retiring from the game.

Although Jack toured Czechoslovakia and Hungary in 1934, he failed to win full England honours. Nevertheless, Jack, who died in 1979, was a talented footballer, whether playing at right or left-back. Strong, determined and intelligent, Jack Milburn is one of the best full-backs in Leeds United's history.

Jim Milburn was the youngest of three brothers to play full-back for Leeds United. Part of an astonishing family, Jim played in the same era as his cousin, Newcastle United legend Jackie Milburn, and was a regular for Leeds when his nephew Jack Charlton joined as an amateur in 1950, although Jim had departed when Jack turned professional.

Born in Ashington on 21 September 1919, Jim, like brother George, began his playing career with Ashington before signing for Leeds in 1935. Unfortunately, his breakthrough into the first team against Sheffield United in September 1939 was the final game before the Second World War, and with his brothers having already moved on, they never played a first-team game together.

Wounded in Belgium, Jim recovered sufficiently to continue his playing career with Leeds in 1946/47. Playing 52 wartime games for Leeds during the hostilities, remarkably, the war years meant that when he played at Preston on the opening day of the season, ten years had elapsed since his joining the club. Jim is the club's only player to have his first two appearances separated by seven years!

Age had caught up with several of his former colleagues and it told on their fitness. Leeds had their worst season since formation with just six victories all season. Relegation was confirmed long before the final matches. Manager Billy Hampson was replaced by former legend Willis Edwards, but Edwards only managed to improve the players' fitness levels. Leeds finished the 1947/48 Second Division campaign in eighteenth place, their lowest placing since formation, which heralded the arrival of Major Frank Buckley.

Surviving Buckley's pre-season clear out and unusual training methods, Jim switched to left-back to accommodate Jimmy Dunn. Nominated penalty taker like brother Jack, Jim scored in victories against Brentford, Lincoln City and Grimbsy Town. Leeds ended the 1948/49 campaign in fifteenth place. In 1949/50 they finished fifth and reached the FA Cup quarter-finals for the first time in the club's history. Having progressed so much, it was somewhat disappointing when they finished fifth again the following season.

Buckley believed there was room for improvement and introduced a number of new players to the team. Jim was one of the casualties with the introduction of Grenville Hair, although he did play a few games at the end of the season as an emergency centre forward, scoring in consecutive home wins against West Ham and Rotherham. Leeds finished the campaign sixth.

Jim's days at Leeds were over and he accepted an offer to join Bradford Park Avenue in June 1952, where he displayed the same commitment in a three-year spell as he had for Leeds during his seventeen-year association with the club before retiring from the game.

Loyal, talented and committed, Jim was smaller in stature than his brothers were, but he was fiercer in his tackling; indeed his ferocity brought him the nickname 'Iron Man'! Jim scored 17 goals in 220 games for Leeds and enabled the Milburn brothers to enjoy a twenty-four-year link with the club. Their deeds are part of Leeds United folklore.

Mike O'Grady joined Leeds United in October 1965, but should have played for his hometown club earlier. Once at Leeds, O'Grady when fit was a dangerous winger and an asset to the side during the club's early trophy successes in the late 1960s.

Born in Leeds on 11 October 1942, as a schoolboy O'Grady starred for Leeds City Boys, so slipping though Leeds' scouting system cost the club a tidy sum. Huddersfield Town weren't as careless and tracked his progress, snapping up the talented winger in 1959.

O'Grady made his Town debut during the 1959/60 season, and went on to give tremendous service for six seasons, making 160 appearances. His early performances won rave reviews and after sixteen games he won the first of 3 England Under-23 caps. Three years after signing professional forms, O'Grady scored twice on his full debut against Northern

Ireland, before being dropped! Nevertheless, he continued to show promise and soon made the short journey across West Yorkshire to Elland Road for £30,000 in October 1965.

Following his debut in a 6-1 victory against Northampton Town, O'Grady impressed during his first season at Elland Road. Quick, elegant, determined, elusive and possessing a terrific shot, O'Grady was immensely dangerous when running at opponents. O'Grady enjoyed the challenge of taking on his opposite number and never got fazed if he lost possession.

A danger domestically, O'Grady immediately made an impact in Europe, scoring a priceless winner in a fourth-round clash in Valencia for a 2-1 aggregate win. His contribution during the season, when Leeds finished runners-up in the League and reached the semi-finals of the Fairs Cup, had been superb.

Unfortunately, after making such an impression, a nasty injury at the beginning of the 1966/67 campaign restricted his appearances. After regaining fitness to play in both legs of the Fairs Cup final against Dynamo Zagreb, another injury wrecked the following season. Months of hard work paid off when O'Grady scored on his comeback at Ipswich Town in August 1969. His appearance resulted in Jimmy Greenhoff moving on, but within weeks, O'Grady was celebrating his first major honour when he helped Leeds clinch the Fairs Cup against Ferencvaros.

The 1968/69 campaign would be O'Grady's most effective for Leeds. Free of injuries, O'Grady missed only four league games and showed Leeds supporters on a sustained basis what he was capable of, and why Revie had signed him. In tandem with Eddie Gray, O'Grady wreaked havoc on defences around the country, creating numerous opportunities for Peter Lorimer and Mick Jones. O'Grady also contributed his share of goals, a solo effort in a crucial 2-1 win against Manchester United during the run-in being particularly memorable. One of the most valuable players during the season that saw Leeds first win the First Division crown, O'Grady's form won a second England cap against France, when he again scored.

Although Leeds had won three trophies in two years, Revie strengthened his squad with the signing of Allan Clarke during the summer. Despite a goal in Leeds' record-breaking 10-0 European Cup win against Lyn Oslo, O'Grady joined Wolves in September 1969 after 120 (+1 substitute) appearances. Sadly, injuries affected spells at Wolves, Birmingham City and Rotherham United prior to his retirement at the end of 1973/74.

But for injuries, O'Grady would surely have achieved greater success. Nevertheless, Leeds United supporters have not forgotten his efforts during the club's early achievements under Don Revie. Mike O'Grady was a terrific talent.

DAVID O'LEARY

David O'Leary succeeded George Graham as manager of Leeds United in September 1998. Blooding a number of youngsters from the club's academy, O'Leary's babes thrilled supporters on the way to two European semi-finals at the onset of the Millennium. Ultimately though, in the modern world of football finance, Leeds' failure to land a Champions League spot in 2001/02 cost O'Leary his job.

Born in Stoke Newington, London on 2 May 1958, O'Leary enjoyed a glorious career at Arsenal for two decades, twice winning the First Division championship, FA Cup and League Cup. A cultured centre-back, O'Leary won 68 caps for the Republic of Ireland and became a national hero in 1990 when he struck the winning spot kick in a penalty shoot-out victory against Romania, enabling his country to reach the World Cup quarter-finals.

Following Arsenal's double FA Cup and League Cup success in 1992/93, Howard Wilkinson persuaded O'Leary to join him at Elland Road during the close season on a free transfer, adding experience to his defence, but after his debut on the opening day of the season at Manchester City the Irishman would play only 10 games due to injury. Retiring as a player in 1995, O'Leary returned to Leeds as George Graham's assistant, before taking the helm as caretaker-manager after Graham's departure to Tottenham Hotspur a few games into the 1998/99 campaign.

After the club failed to land their number-one target, Martin O'Neill, O'Leary was soon in charge on a full-time basis. With Nigel Martyn, Gary Kelly, Lucas Radebe, Lee Bowyer, Ian Harte, Jimmy Floyd Hasselbaink and Harry Kewell in the side, O'Leary galvanised the first team by introducing youngsters such as Alan Smith, Stephen McPhail and Jonathan Woodgate. Suddenly the season was reignited. One defeat in the final fifteen games, including a run of seven successive wins, clinched fifth place and a UEFA Cup spot.

O'Leary had boosted his squad with the arrival of former hero David Batty and Eirik Bakke, and in a memorable 1999/2000 campaign, the players reached the UEFA Cup semi-finals and qualified for the Champions League by finishing third.

At the start of the 2000/01 season, a fine win against TSV Munich 1860 enabled Leeds to play in the Champions League group stages, which they negotiated in style, defeating AC Milan, Lazio and Anderlecht. O'Leary's squad was impressive with Olivier Dacourt, Dominic Matteo, Mark Viduka and Robbie Keane quickly settling and the £18m signing of Rio Ferdinand demonstrated the club's rising ambitions.

The new skipper was in imperious form and scored during a quarter-final win against Deportivo La Coruna, and though Leeds lost to Valencia in the semi-finals, the club was at the dawn of a new era. However, Leeds' failure to qualify for the Champions League when they finished fourth was pressurising club finances. Nevertheless, by January 2002, with Seth Johnson and Robbie Fowler in the side, Leeds sat top of the Premier League, but bad publicity was beginning to engulf the club.

The previous weeks had seen a much-publicised court case involving Lee Bowyer and Jonathan Woodgate concluded. Shortly after the launch of O'Leary's book *Leeds United on Trial,* his expensively assembled side was humbled at Cardiff City in the FA Cup, which heralded a catastrophic two-month period that generated no victories. Although Leeds finished fifth, with no Champions League football on the horizon, the club's 'crown jewels' would have to be sold.

Despite leading Leeds to four consecutive top-five finishes, O'Leary was dismissed before the start of the new campaign. Currently at Aston Villa, O'Leary guided his new charges to a top-six finish in 2003/04 as Leeds succumbed to relegation. Time will tell how supporters view O'Leary's tenure as Leeds United manager. Spending millions, he delivered exhilarating football at times and exceptional nights in Europe, but no trophies. For many fans, his spell is a case of what might have been.

ALAN PEACOCK

Alan Peacock joined Leeds United in February 1964, following an outstanding career with Middlesbrough where he partnered Brian Clough in attack. A prolific goalscorer, Peacock had scored 126 league goals in 218 appearances in addition to winning 4 England caps. At Leeds, he would also make his mark.

Born in Middlesbrough on 29 October 1937, Peacock was the finest header of a ball according to England manager Walter Winterbottom, and had all the attributes to be a great centre forward. Tall, brave and immensely strong in the air, he was a match for any centre-back in his heyday. Don Revie was aware that his team lacked a quality striker and Peacock was his top target even though he was coming towards the end of his playing career. It took a club-record £55,000 fee for Revie to get his man, but it would bring immediate dividends.

Revie's team had begun the 1963/64 campaign well. Indeed, by Christmas they were top, but a poor run of results was affecting confidence. Following a debut goal at Norwich City, it took Peacock a few games to settle but a 3-0 win at Swansea guaranteed promotion, with the new boy grabbing two goals; another Peacock brace in the final game at Charlton tied up the title.

Peacock's input to the campaign had been brief, but his impact alongside Don Weston and Ian Lawson was crucial to the club's title success. Leeds had a cutting edge they had previously lacked in front of goal and Peacock weighed in with 8 goals in 14 appearances.

The move gave Peacock a new lease of life, but he was injury prone and wouldn't figure until the latter stages of the 1964/65 season. Peacock returned to partner Jim Storrie, with the team pushing for the First Division title and FA Cup. Peacock's class proved crucial in a bruising quarter-final clash at Crystal Palace, scoring twice in a 3-0 triumph. Leeds overcame Manchester United to reach the club's first FA Cup final, but ultimately both trophies eluded Leeds.

Peacock's form won him two further caps for England and he was tipped for a place in Alf Ramsey's 1966 World Cup squad. However after scoring Leeds' winning goal in the club's first European match against Torino, an injury just after the New Year wrecked his season and World Cup ambitions. Making nine starts in 1966/67, the arrival of Mick Jones a few weeks into the season signalled an end to Peacock's Leeds career after 31 goals in 65 games. Joining Plymouth in October 1967, within six months Peacock announced his retirement.

Alan Peacock was not just a goalscorer. The target man, he made opportunities for colleagues and was an excellent team player and was one of Revie's most astute signings.

Peacock heads home against Nottingham Forest.

Jimmy Potts joined Leeds United in February 1926 and for eight seasons proved a reliable last line of defence. It was an inconsistent time for Leeds, but Potts is recognised as the club's best pre-war goalkeeper.

Born in Ashington on 25 February 1899, Potts was one of non-league football's star players. Arthur Fairclough was certainly impressed and brought the promising Blyth Spartans 'keeper to Leeds. Fairclough immediately gave Potts his debut at Huddersfield Town, and in his dozen appearances towards the end of the 1925/26 campaign helped Leeds secure their First Division status with four priceless wins.

Unfortunately, throughout their initial spell in the First Division, Leeds had struggled and it was not a surprise when they were relegated in 1926/27. During the close season, Dick Ray replaced Fairclough, and kept faith with the new goalkeeper at the start of the new campaign. Throughout 1927/28, promotion seemed on the cards when two glorious runs underpinned the season. Despite a defeat in the last home game to Manchester City, which cost the title, Leeds finished runners-up. Potts had been sensational and must take a lot of credit for the club-record nine-match unbeaten run near the end of the season when no goals were conceded.

Back in the First Division, after a season of consolidation, Leeds surprised many teams by finishing the 1929/30 campaign in fifth place, their highest placing since formation, and recorded a club-record 8-1 win in the FA Cup against Crystal Palace. Many observers felt Leeds could challenge for the title, but the following term was a disaster. On occasions, Leeds could annihilate opponents but most of the campaign was inconsistent. Relegation was confirmed on the last day of the season.

Once again, the players showed tremendous character and bounced back at the first attempt. Nine consecutive wins in the autumn set them on their way, but poor form during the run-in meant they had to settle for the runners-up spot again. A firm favourite with supporters, the arrival of Stan Moore in 1932 cost Potts his place towards the end of the 1932/33 campaign. With no return in sight, Potts joined Port Vale, serving them diligently for a number of seasons.

Every goalkeeper needs a good understanding with his defenders, and Potts enjoyed it over the years with Willis Edwards, Ernie Hart, Wilf Copping, Bill Menzies and the Milburn brothers. The latter two are not surprising though, because apart from being teammates they came from the same town and Potts was Jack and George Milburn's brother-in-law!

Brave, commanding and a great anticipator of crosses, Potts was a consistent performer for many seasons. An ever-present in his first full campaign, Potts made 262 appearances for Leeds. Experiencing relegation and promotion twice, Jimmy Potts' career at Leeds United was never dull.

LUCAS RADEBE

Lucas Radebe, for the past decade, has been one of Leeds United's most consistent performers since his arrival at the club alongside fellow South African international Phil Masinga for £250,000 in August 1994.

Born in Johannesburg on 12 April 1969, Radebe, one of fourteen children, began his football career with Bophuthatswana as a goalkeeper. Joining ICL Birds, a defensive crisis

resulted in a switch to centre half. One of South Africa's leading sides, Kaiser Chiefs, were so impressed they signed him in 1990. A double winner in 1991/92, Radebe made his South African debut in 1993, the year he finished runner-up in his country's Player of the Year awards.

Leeds boss Howard Wilkinson wasted no time in giving Radebe his debut against Sheffield Wednesday, but a nasty injury after a few games sidelined him until the 1995/96 season when he helped Leeds reach the League Cup final.

One of Wilkinson's most astute signings, Radebe's versatility was an essential element to the team as he could play across the back, in midfield or even as an emergency goalkeeper, which he demonstrated to great effect against Middlesbrough when keeping a clean sheet! However, it is as a central defender that he is best known.

Appointed captain following the departure of Gary McAllister, Radebe is a naturally gifted footballer. One of Europe's leading defenders during the late 1990s, his positional play, strength in the air and temperament made him indispensable to Leeds. Radebe's proudest moment came when he led South Africa to an African Nations Cup triumph in 1996. Skipper of the national team on many occasions, including the 2002 World Cup, Rabebe made 70 appearances on the international stage.

When David O'Leary blooded a number of youngsters in 1998/99, the campaign took off with a number of thrilling victories. Leeds had a tremendous mix of youth and experience and during a memorable season qualified for the Champions League and reached the semi-finals of the UEFA Cup, a campaign that saw Radebe score a crucial late winner against Spartak Moscow, one of only three goals during his years at the club. As Leeds became established as a major force in the Premier League, Radebe's influence as both skipper and a role model helped nurture the likes of Harry Kewell, Ian Harte and Alan Smith.

In recent seasons, however, Rabebe has been plagued by injuries that have restricted his appearances. Missing the 2001/02 campaign, during the past two seasons he has made a return to the first-team set-up following the departure of a number of the side's most promising players due to the club's financial problems.

Last term's relegation to Division One hurt Radebe's pride more than many of his colleagues and he quickly agreed a new deal to play his part as a new era dawned at the club.

A wonderful ambassador for both club and country, Radebe, who made 235 (+25 substitute) appearances for Leeds (to the end of 2003/04), is held in the same esteem as another legendary South African, Albert Johanneson. In an era where club loyalty is a rare commodity, Lucas Radebe has shown the way and been a tremendous servant to Leeds United.

Dick Ray has the unique distinction of being Leeds City's first captain and Leeds United's first manager. He also served the club as a committee member, secretary and assistant manager.

Born in Newcastle-under-Lyme on 4 January 1873, Ray was a cultured left-back for a number of clubs, including Macclesfield Town, Stockport County and Manchester City, before joining City prior to their inaugural season in the Second Division of the Football League in 1905/06.

Playing in the club's first league match against Bradford City on 2 September 1905, Ray helped Leeds finish sixth. In all, Ray made 44 appearances for City, playing his last game against Grimsby Town in 1907, before ending his playing days in non-league football, finally retiring from the game in 1912.

Following the First World War and Leeds City's expulsion from the Football League, Ray was a member of the committee that helped establish Leeds United as the new football team in the city. During the club's debut season in 1919/1920, Ray managed the team. Following a 5-2 win in a friendly against Yorkshire Amateurs, Ray guided the side in the opening half of the Midlands League campaign until Arthur Fairclough's appointment as manager in February 1920.

Fairclough's assistant when Leeds gained entry to the Football League in 1920, Ray wanted to manage in his own right and accepted the managerial post at Doncaster Rovers in June 1923, where he must have created some type of record by signing four brothers: Tom, Harry, Joe and Frank Keetley.

After taking the reigns at Leeds United, his first signing was the youngest Keetley, Charlie, who would go on to become a terrific goal poacher for the club. In his first season at the

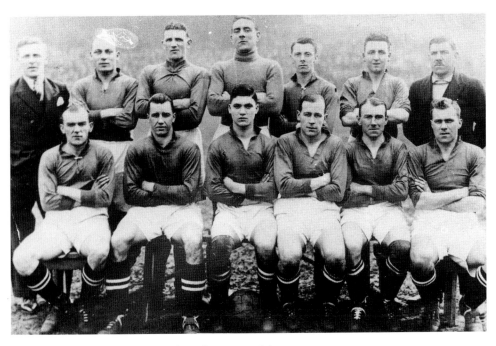

Leeds United c.1931. Dick Ray stands on the extreme right.

Leeds United *c.*1906. Here Ray is seated in the middle row, second from left.

helm Ray guided Leeds into the First Division at the first attempt. Keetley was second-top scorer with 18 goals in just 16 appearances!

Back in the First Division, after a season of consolidation, the team finished fifth; a position not bettered until 1964/65, and recorded a club-record 8-1 win in the FA Cup against Crystal Palace. There was genuine belief that Leeds could challenge for the title but the majority of the 1930/31 campaign was a relegation battle, which was lost on the last day of the season. The following term saw the players bounce back in style, though two wins in the last ten games cost the title.

By the start of the 1932/33 campaign, the team was full of players brought to the club by Ray. Recruiting from the lower leagues and non-league football, Wilf Copping, Billy Furness, Arthur Hydes, George and Jack Milburn and Tom Cochrane were regulars in the starting XI, which says a lot about his eye for a player. In addition, Ray was responsible for putting together one of the best half-back lines in British football during the era: Edwards, Hart and Copping.

As Leeds held their own in the First Division, the highlight a club-record 8-0 win over Leicester City in April 1934, Ray's endeavours were rewarded when he was appointed the first manager of a Football League XI, his team drawing 2-2 against the Scottish League at Ibrox in 1934. The 1934/35 campaign would be anything but comfortable though. Leeds struggled for long periods and with relegation looming Billy Hampson replaced Ray with twelve games remaining. Leeds eventually avoided relegation.

Following his resignation at Leeds, Ray became manager at Bradford City, where he stayed for three years, prior to taking up a scouting post at Millwall for a short period before the outbreak of the Second World War. With the cessation of professional football, Ray started a garage business.

Dick Ray died in 1952 but his efforts on behalf of Leeds City and Leeds United have not been forgotten. Serving both clubs with distinction, seven decades on, a number of his sides' records still stand.

Paul Reaney enjoyed a tremendous career at Leeds United. Blessed with lightning pace, 'Speedy' Reaney was right-back throughout the Don Revie era as Leeds became the team to beat every season.

A strong tackler, superb man-marker and possessing great positional awareness, Reaney was able to monitor the best wingers around. George Best noted during his career that his most difficult games were when facing Reaney. There can be no finer tribute.

Born in London on 22 October 1944, Reaney's family moved to Leeds when he was a few weeks old. A fine sprinter and footballer, Reaney was an apprentice mechanic when he joined the Leeds ground staff in October 1961. Inside a year, Reaney, Gary Sprake and Norman Hunter were thrust into the first team at Swansea Town as Revie began the process of introducing his talented youngsters.

A key member of the team that claimed the Second Division title in 1963/64, Reaney formed a great understanding alongside Willie Bell (replaced by Terry Cooper in 1967), Jack Charlton and Hunter. Revie knew that he had a formidable defensive unit that could cope with the best strikers in the game.

Incredibly consistent and naturally fit, Reaney missed only nine league games up to the 1970 FA Cup final. However, a broken leg sustained at West Ham cost him a place at Wembley and a chance to play at the World Cup finals in Mexico. It was a devastating blow for Reaney, who had represented the Football League on three occasions, won 5 Under-23

Leeds United, September 1968. From left to right, back row: Reaney, Charlton, Madeley, Jones, Harvey, Sprake, Belfitt, Gray, Hunter. Front row: Hibbit, Giles, Cooper, Bremner, O'Grady, Bates, Lorimer, Johanneson.

caps and 2 full caps for England. After making a full recovery he won a third cap in 1971 but his total was a poor return for a player of his class.

Linking superbly with Peter Lorimer down the right flank, Reaney caused havoc for opposing defences with his teasing crosses. One of the most reliable right-backs of his generation, of all his attributes the one that he became renowned for was his goal-line clearances.

It was an uncanny skill, but repeatedly Reaney came up trumps, appearing from nowhere to stop a certain goal. His most important intervention came during the FA Cup final triumph against Arsenal in 1972 when in one of the game's pivotal moments Reaney cleared a certain goal from an Alan Ball strike in the first half.

Winning the First Division championship and Fairs Cup twice, the FA Cup, League Cup and Charity Shield, Reaney also played in two FA Cup finals and all three

European finals; skippering the side against AC Milan in the European Cup Winners' Cup final due to the absence of Billy Bremner through suspension. During this period he was also part of Leeds teams that finished First Division runners-up on five occasions.

A Reaney goal was a rarity. Scoring 9, he was a lucky talisman because following one of his strikes Leeds never lost, winning seven. His first came against Stoke City in an FA Cup tie in March 1963, but most memorably he scored against Manchester United in the final game of 1965/66 and the third match of 1966/67.

Following the departure of Don Revie, it was only a question of time before Reaney moved on. After eighteen seasons at Leeds United, this legendary player decided to join Bradford City in June 1978 before ending his playing career at Newcastle UB United; where he was voted Australia's 'Player of the Year'.

Reaney has run coaching clinics for a number of years and remains involved at Elland Road as part of the corporate hospitality match day team. Playing more FA Cup ties than any other Leeds United player (73), only Bremner and Charlton have made more appearances than this phenomenal footballer. Totalling 736 (+12 substitute) games for Leeds United, Paul Reaney is an all-time great.

Don Revie is a name synonymous with Leeds United. Manager during the club's glory years, Revie converted a team heading for obscurity into one of European football's most feared outfits. Every Leeds manager since has faced comparison, which while understandable, is grossly unfair because the squad that Revie built was a one-off. Appearance-wise, the club's top-ten is filled with Revie's players and the standard of consistency set by his team for a decade will never be equalled.

Born in Middlesbrough on 10 July 1927, Revie began his playing career in 1944 at Leicester City before a £20,000 fee took him to Hull City in 1949. A cultured inside right, within two years Manchester City paid £25,000 for his services. At Maine Road, Revie made his name as a deep-lying centre forward, his distribution skills suiting a system dubbed the 'Revie plan'.

His performances earned him the Football Writers' Player of the Year award in 1954/55. Though City lost the FA Cup final to Newcastle United, Revie starred in his side's 3-1 win over Birmingham City twelve months later. Within eighteen months a £22,000 transfer took Revie to Sunderland, leading them against Leeds in John Charles' final game prior to his move to Juventus in 1957, before ending his playing days at Elland Road after a £12,000 move.

Following his debut in a 3-2 win against Newcastle United, Revie was appointed captain, before passing the honour to Freddie Goodwin after a number of bad results. Playing twice for the Football League representative XI, on the international stage, Revie was unfortunate to win only 6 caps for England. It would be as a manager, however, that he would receive international acclaim, but his entry to the profession had a large slice of luck to begin with.

Nearing the end of the 1960/61 season, thirty-three-year-old Revie applied for the manager's post at Bournemouth. Needing a reference, he asked Leeds director Harry Reynolds to oblige, but while penning the letter, Reynolds realised that Revie was the person Leeds United needed despite his lack of managerial experience. His fellow directors agreed to give Revie a chance and the greatest period in the club's history began.

Initially player-manager, Revie visited Matt Busby at Old Trafford within days of taking the post for advice. His opening game at the helm brought a 3-1 defeat at Portsmouth and the remaining nine games of the season would generate one win, 7-0 against Lincoln City.

Despite the slow progress, Revie persisted with his ideas. Providing the best travel and conditions for his players, Revie changed the club strip to the all-white of Real Madrid and began the process of developing the best youth policy in the country. Following his retirement as a player after 80 games for Leeds, towards the end of his debut season at the helm in 1961/62, his charges were bottom with eleven games left. In need of an experienced campaigner, Revie turned to Bobby Collins.

Revie's hunch worked to perfection as Collins inspired his charges to safety in the final game at Newcastle United. The following term Revie introduced some of his talented youngsters alongside Collins, Jack Charlton, Billy Bremner, Willie Bell and Albert

Left: Don Revie with the League Cup.

Below: Revie, seated, signs for Leeds.

Johanneson. Displaying undoubted potential Gary Sprake, Paul Reaney and Norman Hunter showed their worth in the first team.

Johnny Giles and Alan Peacock's arrival in 1963/64 helped secure the Second Division title and the double was tantalisingly close the following term as Leeds finished runners-up in both League and FA Cup. The next three seasons would see the likes of Terry Cooper, Paul Madeley and Peter Lorimer strengthen the team as Leeds continued to go close to honours, finishing runners-up in the First Division and the Fairs Cup, in addition to reaching the semi-finals of the Fairs Cup and FA Cup.

Revie in action for Leeds

Leeds' pursuit of honours brought accusations of a 'win-at-all-costs' mentality. Some games were brutal and Revie's players did contest refereeing decisions, hustled opponents and were over-zealous at times, but to be dubbed 'dirty Leeds' by the media, a tag that stuck for years, was outrageous.

Tactically astute, Revie's attention to detail was legendary. Producing detailed dossiers on opponents, Revie left nothing to chance. A superb organiser and spotter of talent, Revie's greatest strength was his man-management skills.

Requiring a big squad to battle on all fronts, while the likes of Sprake, Reaney, Cooper, Hunter, Lorimer and Eddie Gray were stalwarts of the side, others such as Mick Bates, David Harvey, Rod Belfitt, Jimmy Greenhoff and Terry Hibbitt were also essential. Good enough to play regularly in the First Division, a number eventually did, each player making significant contributions during the development of the side in the mid-1960s. Balancing the needs of a squad packed with international stars was no easy task, but Revie received absolute loyalty from his players.

At the start of the 1967/68 campaign, Revie strengthened his side by signing Mick Jones. Leeds finally won a major trophy when Cooper's strike against Arsenal secured the League Cup, and Jones grabbed the only goal of the Fairs Cup final against Hungarian giants Ferencvaros to secure the club's first European trophy.

Revie's team was now unstoppable and after five years' endeavour, finally claimed the most coveted domestic prize, the First Division championship in 1968/69 with a record number of points. Revie won the prestigious Manager of the Year award, and with the addition of Allan Clarke prior to the start of the 1969/70 season, Leeds now had the most clinical strike force around.

At the dawn of a new decade, Revie began to remove the defensive shackles on his team and Leeds finally received the plaudits their talents deserved. Securing the Fairs Cup in 1970/71, Revie's boys hit a peak during the second half of the 1971/72 campaign, when their football at times was simply breathtaking.

Inventive, resourceful and dazzling, Leeds produced an awesome display as Manchester United were swept aside 5-1, but the performance that summed up Revie's team's capabilities came in the dying moments of the 7-0 annihilation of Southampton when they kept their opponents at bay with a display of keep-ball.

Sniffer Clarke's diving header secured the FA Cup that term, and with David Harvey, Trevor Cherry, Joe Jordan, Gordon McQueen and Terry Yorath becoming regulars Leeds claimed a second First Division title in 1973/74, a season when they went twenty-nine games undefeated from the start of the campaign.

Although Leeds won six major trophies, more than any other team, between 1968 and 1974, they should have claimed more. First Division runners-up five times, FA Cup runners-up on three occasions, losing finalists in the Fairs Cup and European Cup Winners' Cup, their most trying season came in 1969/70 when only fatigue and fixture congestion denied them a unique League, FA Cup and European Cup treble.

Nevertheless, Revie's boys always finished in the top four of the First Division and were the team to beat every season. Playing to packed houses, they were the most talked-about and written-about club in domestic football. Revie's side is the greatest in the club's history and his team set standards that others have attempted to match. It had been an incredible journey for Revie and his players but it was time for the greatest manager in the club's history to move on after a glorious decade of success.

Revie accepted the challenge of managing England in July 1974 but, despite capping many players, was unable to recreate the 'club' atmosphere at international level he desired. After initially improving results, when qualification to the 1978 World Cup was out of reach, Revie accepted a lucrative job to coach the United Arab Emirates, amid rumours of his imminent sacking by the Football Association.

Announcing his decision in the *Daily Mail* before informing FA officials, Revie was heavily criticised by his former employers and the media. The FA imposed a ban on Revie from working in England, which Revie successfully overturned, but the former England manager's reputation never recovered nationally. Apart from a consulting role at Leeds, Revie never managed another league club.

When Don Revie died in May 1989 of motor neurone disease, the city of Leeds mourned. The greatest manager in the club's history, Revie, awarded the OBE in 1970, put Leeds United on the football map worldwide and made household names of his star players.

One can speculate how many trophies Leeds may have claimed if Revie had allowed his team to be more adventurous earlier or brought the more reliable Harvey in for Sprake sooner than he did. However, despite being excessively superstitious and over-estimating opponents his team was more than capable of comfortably defeating at times, nobody can citicise Revie's achievements because no manager before or since at Elland Road has come close to matching his success.

Three decades on, Revie's legendary side is acknowledged as one of the greatest ever post-war teams and memories of his outstanding team live on in numerous videos and DVDs. However, the true test of what this remarkable manager achieved is to speak to football supporters around the globe. Wherever you go, all can name player-by-player the great Leeds United side that Revie built. That is Don Revie's legacy.

HARRY REYNOLDS

Far left: Chairman Harry Reynolds pictured with Don Revie, Bob English and Les Cocker.

Harry Reynolds holds a special place in the history of Leeds United Football Club because without his foresight Don Revie might have been allowed to leave in March 1961. If Revie had, one can only speculate what direction the club would have taken. Leeds needed a shake up from top to bottom and Reynolds knew it.

A self-made millionaire with no formal education, Reynolds began his working life as a Leeds Co-op flour boy before working for the railways and as a fireman prior to building up an engineering and steel stockholding company. A successful industrialist, Reynolds was managing director of H.L. Reynolds Engineers and Steel Erectors before stepping down in 1959.

Nearing the end of the 1960/61 campaign Revie realised his playing days were coming to an end and asked Reynolds for a reference as he wanted to apply for the job of manager at Bournemouth. While penning the document Reynolds recognised that Revie was just the person Leeds United required, despite his lack of managerial experience, so he tore up the letter. Revie was young, full of ideas, enthusiastic and knew how he wanted to take the club forward. Reynolds persuaded his fellow directors to give Revie a chance, heralding the greatest period in the club's history.

In December 1961, Reynolds, who played for Leeds Schoolboys and had joined the board in 1955, succeeded Sam Bolton as club chairman. Funds were made available for Revie; £50,000 from Reynolds, £10,000 from the other directors. A people person, Reynolds made everyone at the club feel important, from players' wives to ground staff, cleaners and tea ladies. On match days he would sell raffle tickets and sort out problems for supporters. As for the players, they travelled everywhere first class. Nothing was left to chance.

The importance of the club's youth system was paramount in Revie's strategy. If Revie wanted a player Reynolds ensured it happened. On frequent long-distance trips in search of talent with Revie, Reynolds' charisma persuaded parents that their sons would be looked after by Leeds United. It didn't matter that larger clubs were also interested; Reynolds out-thought them. Within two years of Reynolds becoming chairman the likes of Paul Madeley, Peter Lorimer and Eddie Gray had all arrived at Leeds. The club would benefit for years to come.

Reynolds' behind-the-scenes role cannot be underestimated. By the time he resigned through ill-health in August 1967, the club's £150,000 debts had been turned into a profit, but far more importantly, before his death in September 1974, Reynolds' and Revie's dreams of major honours had been fulfilled. Harry Reynolds' endeavour on behalf of Leeds United was quite rightly honoured when he was appointed a life vice-president at the club in 1967.

Andy Ritchie became a firm favourite with Leeds United supporters during his four seasons at the club in the mid–1980s. Leeds fans were fully aware of his talent as a striker because as a teenager he struck a hat-trick for Manchester United against Leeds at Old Trafford in 1979! Although not a prolific goalscorer while at Elland Road, Ritchie was hard-working, skilful and grabbed his share of goals.

Born in Manchester on 28 November 1960, Ritchie was a star with England Schoolboys before turning professional for his hometown club in 1979. After hitting the headlines against Leeds, Ritchie seemed set for a promising career at Old Trafford but was soon on his way to Brighton for £500,000 after less than two seasons. In March 1983, after gaining an England Under-21 cap, a swap deal with Terry Connor brought Ritchie to Yorkshire.

Ritchie (centre) celebrates a goal.

As Eddie Gray began the process of rebuilding Leeds in the Second Division, Ritchie was one of Gray's first signings and replaced Frank Worthington at centre forward. The new number nine got off to flyer on his debut with the opening goal in a 2-1 win against Crystal Palace. Leeds ended the season eighth.

Leeds made an atrocious start to the 1983/84 campaign that saw them languishing near the foot of the table by Christmas but slowly, with the introduction of Tommy Wright, Scott Sellars and veteran Peter Lorimer, Leeds pulled clear. John Sheridan's return from injury the following term brought balance to the side and Leeds produced some majestic football as Gray's team tried to play their way out of the Second Division.

Ritchie was in fine form early on, scoring hat-tricks against Oldham Athletic 6-0 and Wimbledon 5-2, and a brace against Shrewsbury, but one goal after the New Year resulted in Gray signing Ian Baird. One more strike came Ritchie's way when Baird was injured, but his days at centre forward for Leeds were over.

Out of favour at the start of 1985/86, following Billy Bremner's appointment in October 1985, Ritchie returned to the side reinvigorated. Revelling in his new role on the right flank, Ritchie's touch, football brain and accurate shooting brought a scoring frenzy towards the end of the season with eight goals in the last nine games. Leeds finished mid-table but the following term there would be no thoughts of mediocrity as the club battled for promotion and reached the semi-finals of the FA Cup.

Although in dispute with the club over his contract, Ritchie featured for much of the campaign, notching crucial goals in victories against Reading, Hull City, Portsmouth, Oldham Athletic, Grimsby Town and Millwall. However, an injury sustained towards the end of the season meant he could only play in two of the play-off matches, including the final against Charlton Athletic when, heartbreakingly, two goals in the dying moments crushed Leeds' promotion hopes.

During the close season Ritchie moved to Oldham for £50,000. It would prove a bargain for the Latics. Scoring freely, Ritchie was a key player in the side that reached a League Cup final, FA Cup semi-final and won the Second Division title in 1990/91. Struggling with injuries, Ritchie joined Scarborough in 1995 for a brief spell.

Since his retirement as a player Ritchie managed Oldham before returning to Elland Road in 2002 as director of the Leeds United Football Academy. Highly regarded as a coach, the likes of current stars Matthew Kilgallon and Frazer Richardson have already benefited from his experience. A talented footballer, Andy Ritchie scored 44 goals in 149 (+10 substitute) games for Leeds during a traumatic period in the club's history.

John Sheridan was the star player at Leeds United for a number of years following his arrival at Elland Road in 1982. In an era when success was at a premium, Sheridan's endeavours gave fans hope that the good times would return.

Born in Manchester on 1 October 1964, Sheridan was a talented teenager but failed to make the grade at Manchester City before building a reputation as a quality midfield player under three Leeds legends. Taken on by Allan Clarke, Eddie Gray gave Sheridan his debut against Middlesbrough in November 1982 and Billy Bremner built his side around the playmaker as Leeds attempted to win back their First Division status.

Regarded as the best midfield player in the lower leagues, although prone to the odd reckless tackle, Sheridan impressed with his composure, long-range passing ability, close control and eye for goal with spectacular shots. Recovering from a broken leg, which caused him to miss much of the 1983/84 season, Sheridan returned to produce some majestic football alongside Scott Sellars, Tommy Wright and Andy Ritchie as Gray's team attempted to play their way out of the Second Division. During 1984/85, Sheridan grabbed goals in thumping wins against Oldham Athletic 6-0, Crystal Palace 4-1 and Notts County 5-0 but inconsistency saw Leeds finish seventh.

Sheridan's most memorable campaign for Leeds was in 1986/87 when Bremner's side challenged for promotion and reached the semi-finals of the FA Cup. Prompting from midfield, Sheridan was at the centre of everything. An expert at set pieces; he was also first-choice penalty taker. Scoring six times from the spot, Sheridan struck in victories against Crystal Palace, Portsmouth and Plymouth Argyle, but his most important conversion came against West Brom when a 3-2 win guaranteed fourth place and a shot at the end-of-season play-offs.

After accounting for Oldham Athletic, Sheridan scored a sensational free-kick against Charlton Athletic in the play-off final. Heartbreakingly, two goals in the dying moments destroyed everyone's dreams. Finishing joint-top scorer with 15 league goals, he deservedly won the supporters' Player of the Year award, but it was scant consolation. The huge disappointment lingered into 1987/88. Although pre-season favourites, it took until December to mount a challenge with six consecutive victories. However, further unpredictability saw Leeds miss out on the play-offs.

When Howard Wilkinson replaced Bremner, Sheridan's form suffered and his days at Elland Road were numbered. In August 1989, Leeds accepted a £650,000 bid from Nottingham Forest, giving Sheridan a chance to play in the First Division but, after 1 appearance for Brian Clough, a £500,000 transfer took him back to the Second Division with Sheffield Wednesday.

Settling immediately, Sheridan became a firm favourite at Wednesday and entered club folklore in 1991 when he scored the only goal of a memorable League Cup final triumph over Manchester United, the club's first major honour since 1935. In 1993, Sheridan collected runners-up medals in the FA Cup and League Cup. Playing 244 games for Wednesday, Sheridan went on to enjoy brief spells at a number of clubs.

In the international arena, Sheridan represented the Republic of Ireland at Youth, Under-21 and Under-23 level before making his full debut in March 1988 against Romania. Winning 34 caps, Sheridan was a member of his country's 1988 European Championship, 1990 and 1994 World Cup squads.

John Sheridan was immensely popular with Leeds United supporters throughout his years at the club. In 261 (+6 substitute) appearances, Sheridan scored 52 goals, many memorable, and was the danger man of the side during a difficult era in the club's history.

Leeds United, 1988/89. From left to right, back row: Aspin, Ashurst, Grayson, Day, Haddock, Swan, Blake, Rennie. Middle row: Ormsby, Aizlewood, Sheridan, Davison, Sinclair, Williams, Taylor, Maguire, Noteman, Mumby. Front row: Smith, Speed, Pearson, Adams, Snodin, Bremner (manager), Batty, Hilaire, Baird, Stiles, Brockie.

Alan Smith made a dream debut for Leeds United when he scored within minutes of coming on as a substitute at Liverpool in November 1998. For the seventeen-year old local lad from Rothwell it was a sensational start; his strike inspired an impressive 3-1 win and announced his arrival on the Premiership scene.

Born in Leeds on 28 October 1980, Smith was one of a number of youngsters new boss David O'Leary pitched into the first team. Playing for Leeds meant everything to Smith and supporters were quick to embrace a new hero who played with pride, passion and total commitment in every game.

Smith scored in a thrilling 4-1 win against Charlton Athletic on his home debut and, with Leeds losing once in the last fourteen games of the 1998/99 campaign, a new era had dawned at Elland Road. The Rothwell youngster was very much part of the future.

Used sparingly the following term, Smith helped Leeds reach the semi-finals of the UEFA Cup, scoring against Lokomotiv Moscow, but he began the 2000/01 campaign in blistering form with a number of goals, including a crucial strike at TSV Munich 1860 in the Champions League preliminary round to secure Leeds' place in Europe's premier competition.

On the European stage, Smith was a revelation. Linking brilliantly with Mark Viduka, Leeds raced through the group stages. Among notable strikes, Smith's goal at Lazio and delicate chip against Anderlecht were particularly special. Sadly, his temperament caught up with him in the semi-final defeat to Valencia when he was sent off, but even that could not detract from a remarkable campaign for the young striker who finished second-top scorer behind Viduka with 18 goals, scoring braces in the Premier League against Everton, Tottenham Hotspur and Leicester City.

One of the brightest prospects in English football, having played for England at Under-21 level, Smith made his full international debut against Mexico to cap a memorable season. Smith's fiery nature is a major part of his game but it resulted in a number of dismissals for Leeds. His tendency to make rash challenges and react to provocation has brought red cards at representative level for England also, most recently in a Euro 2004 qualifier against Macedonia. Aggression is fine but it must be controlled if Smith is to develop on the world stage.

Sadly, the past three seasons have seen a rapid decline in the club's fortunes as finances spiralled out of control, but throughout the most difficult period in the club's history, which has seen numerous managerial changes, Smith battled away.

Although not the most prolific of strikers, in 2002/03 Smith became only the second Leeds player to score four goals in a European tie following a 4-1 victory against Hapoel Tel Aviv, and his efforts last season saw him deservedly win the club's Player of the Year award. His distress at relegation summed up what the club meant to him and captaining the side in the final game of the season against Charlton was a fitting tribute to a player who always gives everything in every game.

There can be no doubt Smith cherished his years at Leeds, but his £7m move to Manchester United during the close season devastated his many followers at Elland Road. Leeds stars have taken the trip across the Pennines to Old Trafford before, but Smith's transfer was emotionally viewed as being on a different scale to previous ones. Scoring 56 goals in 190 (+30 substitute) appearances for Leeds, fans hope they have not seen Alan Smith wear the white shirt of Leeds United for the last time, because in the last decade there has been no prouder footballer than when Smith played for his hometown club.

GARY SPEED

Gary Speed made his debut for Leeds United at nineteen and quickly secured his place in the side on the left side of midfield. Blessed with natural pace, vision and an eye for goal, he became a firm favourite with supporters.

Born Mancot, North Wales, on 8 September 1969, Howard Wilkinson gave Speed his debut in the penultimate match of the 1988/89 season at Oldham, but during the early months of the 1989/90 Second Division campaign only utilised him as a substitute. With a third of the campaign to go Wilkinson gave Speed his first start at Oxford. Leeds overturned a 2-0 deficit to win 4-2 and Speed retained his place in the side, scoring crucial goals against Bradford City, Sheffield United and Brighton. Speed received much credit for his performances during the run-in to the Second Division title.

In his inaugural season in top-flight football, Speed featured in every League and cup match as Leeds finished fourth in the First Division and reached the semi-finals of the League Cup. Finishing with 10 goals in all competitions, including one at Everton on the opening day of the season, Speed was one of the brightest prospects around. It had been an amazing turnaround in the club's fortunes, but the new campaign would bring even more excitement as Leeds took on Manchester United head-to-head for the biggest prize in domestic football in 1991/92.

Speed in action against Luton.

During an amazing season, Speed formed a superb partnership alongside Gordon Strachan, Gary McAllister and David Batty in midfield. Throughout the league campaign, there were many twists and turns but in a dramatic finale, Leeds held their nerve to clinch the First Division Championship with a game to spare. Missing only one match, Speed scored 7 league goals, including a humdinger at Southampton. He also filled in at left-back for a few games in Tony Dorigo's absence.

Exceptional in the air, this talented footballer could out-jump and out-hang taller players. Particularly effective at set pieces, the Welshman perfected his timing to lose markers and finish off moves with a clinical strike. Speed played in Leeds' thrilling 4–3 win in the Charity Shield over Liverpool at Wembley, but the 1992/93 league campaign was a disaster as Leeds failed to win an away game all season and only just avoided relegation. Second top scorer with 12 goals, Speed's strikes against Aston Villa, Southampton, Sheffield United and Sheffield Wednesday gained crucial points during a traumatic term.

Leeds got back on track over the next couple of seasons, and Speed continued to score his share of goals. Joint-second-top scorer in 1993/94 with 12 goals, including a brace against Wimbledon, two fifth-place finishes saw Leeds qualify for the UEFA Cup but the 1995/96 season again ended in bitter disappointment, despite reaching the Coca-Cola Cup final and the quarter-finals of the FA Cup. Chipping in with valuable goals through a troubled season, although Leeds lost out at Wembley, Speed was top scorer in the competition with winners against Notts County, Derby County and Reading. The latter strike would prove to be his last for the club.

At the end of the season, after 291 (+20 substitute) appearances and 57 goals for the club, Speed decided to join Everton in a £3 million transfer, but failed to settle at Goodison Park, and after just over a season joined Newcastle United, where he regained his form. Teaming up with David Batty, Speed helped Newcastle to consecutive FA Cup finals and having now completed seven seasons at the club is one of the few players to play in every Premier League campaign. He joined Bolton Wanderers before the start of the 2004/05 season.

Making his international bow against Costa Rica in 1990, Speed won 85 caps, placing him second on the all-time list for his country. Skipper on numerous occasions, he was bitterly disappointed when Wales failed to overhaul Russia in a Euro 2004 play off match last term.

Gary Speed has enjoyed a wonderful career in the game since making the grade at Leeds United. Despite his success at other clubs, Leeds followers will remember this talented Welshman for his goals and consistent performances during the club's renaissance in the early 1990s.

GARY SPRAKE

Gary Sprake made a dramatic entry to senior football for Leeds United at the age of sixteen when he was called up as a last-minute replacement for goalkeeper Tommy Younger against Southampton in March 1962. With the squad on the South Coast, Leeds' apprentice keeper flew down on the day of the match and only just made the kick-off. The match ended in a 4-1 defeat but Sprake was soon an ever-present as Don Revie began the process of producing Leeds United's greatest ever team.

Born in Winchwen, near Swansea, on 3 April 1945, Sprake grew up close to legendary Welsh goalkeeper Jack Kelsey. A schoolboy star, the budding 'keeper joined Leeds' band of youngsters at Elland Road being groomed for stardom. Turning professional two months after making his debut, Revie played Sprake, Paul Reaney and Norman Hunter at Swansea Town in September 1962. All three would become legends, and alongside Willie Bell, replaced by

Sprake clears his lines with help from Terry Cooper.

Terry Cooper in August 1967, and Jack Charlton, Leeds had a defensive unit that would cope with the best strikers around.

A key member of the 1963/64 side that secured the Second Division title, Sprake would be Revie's number-one 'keeper as Leeds claimed the First Division Championship with a record number of points in 1968/69 (the only campaign when he was ever present), the League Cup in 1967/68 and the Fairs Cup twice, 1967/68 and 1970/71. The most consistent team around, Sprake was also in goal when Leeds finished runners-up in the league on five occasions, reached two FA Cup finals and a Fairs Cup final during a sensational period.

Generally, Sprake was a model of consistency but he did make the occasional 'howler' in high-profile televised games. His most embarrassing clanger came at Anfield in 1966 when he threw the ball into his own net. The Liverpool Kop immediately sang 'Careless Hands'! Against Everton in an FA Cup semi-final his error cost the only goal of the game, as it did in the last minute of a league clash against Crystal Palace in 1970. However, Sprake's worst mistake came against Chelsea in the 1970 FA Cup final at Wembley when, with Leeds in control, Sprake let in a soft equaliser just before the half-time interval.

The occasional lapse apart, Sprake was one of the best 'keepers around during the late 1960s and early 1970s. He needed to be because David Harvey was an outstanding deputy. Blessed with natural ability, Sprake anticipated trouble, was a terrific shot-stopper, often inspirational and won many games for Leeds. His best performance came in Budapest in the Fairs Cup final second leg against Ferencvaros when Leeds clinched the trophy for the first time. Sprake was outstanding and pulled off a number of world-class saves.

The watershed in Sprake's career came during the 1971/72 season when Revie preferred Harvey to his more experienced goalkeeper in the semi-finals of the FA Cup. As Leeds went on to claim the only domestic honour to elude them, Sprake was a non-playing reserve and realised his days at Leeds were over after missing just 41 out of 420 league encounters following his debut a decade earlier. Following a brief spell at Birmingham City, Sprake retired through injury in 1975.

On the international stage, Sprake became Wales' youngest 'keeper when he faced Scotland in 1964 aged eighteen and went on to win 37 caps over an eleven-year period. When evaluating his career at Leeds United, Gary Sprake had more good games than bad ones, but his lack of concentration at crucial moments cost Leeds dearly.

Supporters will always wonder whether Leeds would have won more trophies had Revie switched Harvey and Sprake earlier, but the record books state that this talented Welshman played in goal for Leeds more than any other goalkeeper. Ninth on the all-time list, Sprake made a total of 505 (+2 substitute) appearances for the club.

MEL STERLAND

Mel Sterland was an immensely popular player for Leeds United during the club's renaissance in the early 1990s. A swashbuckling attacking right-back, Sterland arrived at Elland Road in July 1989. Dubbed 'Zico' due to a booming shot that brought him spectacular goals, Sterland would prove to be a shrewd investment.

Born in Sheffield on 1 October 1961, former Leeds legend Jack Charlton gave Sterland his Sheffield Wednesday debut in 1979 before he enhanced his reputation under future Leeds boss Howard Wilkinson. After a decade at Hillsborough, where he won an England cap against Saudi Arabia, Sterland joined Rangers for a club record £800,000, but failed to settle in Scotland despite gaining a Championship medal and returned south to play for his former manager by the start of the 1989/90 campaign.

An immediate hit on his debut in the opening game of the season at Newcastle United, supporters loved his enthusiasm and commitment in every game. On occasions Sterland got caught for pace, but a strong tackler and anticipator of trouble, he would always look to support the attack with surging runs down the right flank, and created numerous goals with pinpoint crosses. Ian Baird, Bobby Davison and Lee Chapman all benefited during the season; Baird's flying header against Newcastle United, following a typical Sterland assist, was particularly memorable.

Sterland's prowess at the long throw also caused havoc for defences and he chipped in with 5 goals, each gaining valuable points. His thirty-yard thunderbolt at Sheffield United was special, but his most important strike came in the penultimate game of the campaign at home to Leicester City, which set Leeds on the way to a 2-1 win. Leeds clinched promotion and the title a week later at Bournemouth, amid unforgettable scenes, and Sterland was back in top-flight football.

A regular during Leeds' 1990/91 campaign, when he again scored five times, Sterland remained a key player in the side as Leeds went for the Championship in 1991/92. Notching 6 league goals, his best return at Leeds, Sterland's spot kick against Manchester United denied Sir Alex Ferguson's team a crucial away win prior to New Year, and enabled Leeds to stay in the hunt for the title.

In an amazing campaign, two of Sterland's best performances came in televised clashes as Leeds thumped Aston Villa 4-1 and Sheffield Wednesday 6-1. The win at Wednesday was particularly sweet as it was Sterland's first game back at his hometown club. Unfortunately, an ankle injury denied Sterland the chance of playing during the run-in to the title, but he won a deserved Championship medal.

It had been an astonishing turnaround in the club's fortunes, and Sterland had played his part, but the following term Sterland's injury would see him make only five appearances before retiring from the professional game in 1994. Player-manager of Boston United for two years, Sterland now works in the media with Radio Aire.

Mel Sterland played 143 (+3 substitute) games for Leeds United as the club finally came out of a terrible period in their history. Continually motivating players around him, Sterland enjoyed a wonderful rapport with supporters. A crowd-pleaser, fans loved his gestures after a trademark goal. Despite playing only three full seasons at Elland Road, Zico made his mark during the club's climb back to the pinnacle of English football.

Sterland scores a crucial equaliser against Manchester United during the 1991/92 campaign.

JIM STORRIE

Jim Storrie was one of Don Revie's best early signings for the club in June 1962 after Leeds miraculously avoided being relegated in 1961/62. Desperate for a centre forward who could deliver after the shenanigans of the previous campaign when Jack Charlton played as an emergency centre forward, Revie's £15,000 investment would prove to be a bargain as Leeds became a force to be reckoned with in the First Division.

Born in Kirkintilloch, Lanarkshire, on 31 March 1940, Storrie was a prolific goalscorer in Scottish football for Airdrie and made an immediate impact following his move to Elland Road. Scoring the only goal against Stoke City on the opening day of the 1962/63 season, Storrie led the line as Leeds finished fifth in the Second Division. Strong and well-built, Storrie finished the season as top scorer with 25 league goals, which included hat tricks against Plymouth Argyle and Cardiff City.

To place Storrie's effort in context, in the club's history it is interesting to note that only Tom Jennings (1926/27) and John Charles (1952/53, 1953/54, 1955/56 and 1956/57) have bettered his total of league goals in a campaign. Similarly, three decades on since Storrie notched 27 goals in all competitions only Peter Lorimer (1967/68 and 1971/72) and Lee Chapman (1990/91) have accumulated more goals in one season.

Revie was delighted with his purchase, but nine games into the 1963/64 campaign, a niggling injury meant Storrie could only start fifteen games of the Second Division title campaign. Recovering during the close season, Storrie was raring to go in the First Division and again finished top scorer with 19 goals, notching braces against Wolves, Fulham and Stoke City as Revie's aces stunned pundits by finishing League runners-up behind

Storrie strikes a goal for Leeds.

Leeds United's 1965 FA Cup final side. From left to right, back row: Hunter, Charlton, Sprake, Reaney, Bell. Front row: Giles, Storrie, Peacock, Revie (manager), Collins, Johanneson, Bremner.

Manchester United. In the FA Cup, Storrie scored against Everton and Crystal Palace as Leeds reached Wembley for the first time in the club's history.

Injured during the opening two months of 1965/66, Storrie bounced back to finish the campaign second-top scorer behind Peter Lorimer. Hard working and determined, his foraging forced defenders into errors, from which both Storrie and his colleagues benefited. Once again, Leeds finished runners-up in the First Division and in their first tilt at the Fairs Cup reached the semi-finals. Storrie scored against Ujpest Dosza, but it would be his only European goal due to the form of emerging stars such as Lorimer, Jimmy Greenhoff and Eddie Gray.

Making just three starts in 1966/67, Storrie joined Aberdeen in February 1967. In a ten-month spell, Storrie helped the Dons reach the Scottish Cup final but missed a penalty in his side's 2-0 defeat to Celtic. Within months, Storrie began a two-year spell at Rotherham United before moving to Portsmouth where he played until 1972. Following a loan spell with Aldershot, Storrie was player-coach at St Mirren and player-manager at Waterlooville. Storrie returned to his roots as a coach at Airdrie prior to becoming manager of St Johnstone.

Jim Storrie scored 67 goals in 153 (+3 substitute) appearances for Leeds United. An unsung hero, Storrie played an important role in the development of Revie's side for four years during the mid-1960s. Top scorer between 1963 and 1966, Storrie's nearest challenger was Albert Johanneson during the same period with 43 goals. Revie's intuitive purchase more than paid back his transfer fee.

GORDON STRACHAN

Gordon Strachan was the principal driving force behind Leeds United's renaissance in the early 1990s. Nobody could have predicted how successful Leeds would become with Strachan leading the side, but it was a remarkable period after Howard Wilkinson persuaded the thirty-two-year-old Scot to sign for £300,000 in March 1989.

Born in Edinburgh on 9 February 1957, Strachan began his playing career with Dundee, before a £50,000 transfer took him to Aberdeen in 1977. During seven seasons, Strachan helped the Dons break the domination of Celtic and Rangers, winning two Scottish League titles, three consecutive Scottish Cups and the European Cup Winners' Cup. Voted Scottish Player of the Year in 1979/80, Strachan joined Manchester United in August 1984 for £500,000 and won an FA Cup winners' medal in his first season, but was ready for a new challenge by 1988/89.

Making an instant impact on his debut against Portsmouth, Strachan's enthusiasm, boundless energy, considerable footballing skills and drive inspired everyone around him at the club. Leeds finished the season comfortably in mid-table, but Wilkinson and Strachan's aspirations were far higher. After eight years in the wilderness, the sole target was to bring top-flight football back to Elland Road.

Leeds overcame a slow start to top the table by New Year. With his darting runs from the right side of midfield, Strachan was at the hub of everything positive and fans began to believe that finally this could be Leeds' season. Despite having a substantial points lead eroded during the second half of the season, in a nail-biting finish Leeds secured promotion and the Second Division title in the last game at Bournemouth.

The key player throughout the campaign was undoubtedly Strachan. Top scorer with 16 league goals, including seven penalties and a hat-trick against Swindon Town, if one moment typified the skipper's season it was a wonderful strike in the closing minutes of Leeds' penultimate game of the season at home to Leicester City. With the scores level and tension unbearable, no supporter present will ever forget the relief and excitement when Strachan's sensational eighteen-yard strike flew into the net.

The first year back in the First Division would see Leeds surpass everyone's expectations by finishing fourth and reaching the semi-finals of the League Cup. Strachan would return to the Scotland side and win the prestigious Footballer of the Year award, completing a rare double, having won the Scottish equivalent.

Playing for his country after an absence of eighteen months was particularly special for Strachan. A regular in Scotland's team since making his debut against Northern Ireland in 1980, Strachan had represented his country in the 1982 and 1986 World Cup finals. His comeback would enable this proud Scot to win 50 caps before retiring from international competition.

GORDON STRACHAN

Gordon Strachan shows the the League
Championship Trophy to fans.

Considered dark horses for the 1991/92 championship, no pundit predicted the head-to-head battle that would ensue between Leeds and Manchester United. In Strachan, Gary McAllister, David Batty and Gary Speed, Leeds had the best midfield in the country and possessed balance throughout the side. There were many twists and turns, and some notable performances by Leeds, especially fine away wins at Aston Villa and Sheffield Wednesday, but it would not be until the Easter fixtures that Leeds edged ahead decisively to clinch the title following a dramatic 3-2 win at Sheffield United with a game to spare.

Playing 35 games, Strachan was sensational. Demanding absolute effort from everyone, Strachan's leadership skills stood out. A superb reader of the game, the Scot held his nerve to convert four penalties in the opening six games, including a brace at Southampton.

During the latter stages of the season, Strachan suffered with sciatica and some people feared he might not play again. However, this remarkable character recovered to appear in Leeds' Charity Shield win against Liverpool at Wembley, but the 1992/93 league campaign was almost a disaster as Leeds failed to win an away game and only just avoided relegation. At the end of a troubled season, Strachan was deservedly voted the club's Player of the Year, providing the highlights with a brilliant strike against Vfb Stuttgart in a European Cup clash and a treble against Blackburn Rovers.

Indispensable to the side, Strachan led Leeds for two more years during the Indian summer of his career. Awarded an OBE, Strachan joined Coventry City in March 1995 before taking the helm from Ron Atkinson. After a number of relegation battles, the Sky Blues finally succumbed in 2000/01. Leaving Coventry a few games into the new campaign, Strachan guided Southampton to the FA Cup final in 2003. Respected among his peers, Strachan surprised many pundits last season when he decided to take a break from the game.

Scoring 45 goals in his 234 (+10 substitute) appearances for Leeds United, Strachan's impact at the club is akin to Bobby Collins, another fiery Scot who led the side with distinction in the 1960s. Leading by example, Gordon Strachan is the most influential player since the Don Revie era and one of the best signings in the club's history.

BOBBY TURNBULL

Bobby Turnbull was one of the most dangerous outside rights around following his arrival at Leeds United in May 1925. Quickly breaking into the first team, Turnbull proved to be an excellent acquisition by manager Arthur Fairclough.

Born in South Bank, near Middlesbrough, on 17 December 1895, Bradford Park Avenue signed Turnbull after he impressed as a last-minute replacement against his hometown club in a testimonial match. A consistent performer for Avenue, Turnbull's performances won him an England cap against Northern Ireland in 1920, and a place on the Football Association's tour of South Africa the following year.

Arriving at Leeds just before his thirtieth birthday, Turnbull went on to play 215 games but it would be his goal-making abilities which would make this tricky winger invaluable with Tom Jennings, Charlie Keetley and Russell Wainscoat all benefiting from his skills.

Following his debut against Notts County on the opening day of the 1925/26 season, Turnbull opened his Leeds account with a brace at Leicester City in a 3-1 win. Throughout their initial stay in the First Division Leeds struggled, and but for a 4-1 win on the last day of the league campaign against Tottenham Hotspur, when Turnbull opening the scoring, would have been relegated.

The inevitable did occur in 1926/27. Turnbull scored three goals in the final six games, including a strike against West Ham United in the last home game of the season, but it was far too late. With only three victories after the turn of the year, Leeds were back in the Second Division.

Dick Ray became manager and Leeds began the new campaign well. Two unbeaten runs underpinned the promotion drive. A defeat in the last home game cost the title but Leeds finished as Second Division runners-up. Turnbull was again among the goals, notching 8, including a brace in a 6-2 win against Reading, and was something of a lucky talisman because all his goals came in games that Leeds won, including handsome wins against Swansea Town 5-0, Stoke City 5-1 and Notts County 6-0.

Back in the First Division, after a season of consolidation Leeds finished fifth, a position not bettered for three decades, and recorded a club-record 8-1 win against Crystal Palace in the FA Cup. Turnbull grabbed a goal in the record-breaking match and would have his most prolific season in 1930/31 when there was genuine belief that Leeds could challenge for the title.

Unfortunately, the campaign was a relegation dogfight despite thumping wins against Middlesbrough 7-0 and Manchester United 5-0; a match in which Turnbull grabbed his only hat-trick for the club, one of only two Leeds players to record a treble against their Pennine rivals. Relegation arrived in the final game in spite of a 3-1 win against Derby County. As Leeds bounced back the following term, Turnbull was out of the first-team frame. Playing one game in 1931/32, Turnbull joined Rhyl and retired in 1933.

Bobby Turnbull, who died in 1952, was an excellent player for Leeds United. Apart from making countless goals for his colleagues, he had an impressive strike rate, notching 46 goals. During his six years at the club, Turnbull excited and entertained the Elland Road faithful.

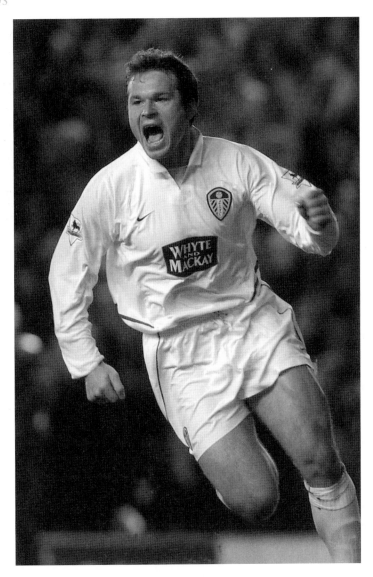

M ark Viduka has been Leeds United's focal point in attack during the highs and lows of
the past four seasons. Despite not possessing searing pace, his upper-body strength,
touch on the ball and predatory instincts have made him one of Europe's most sought-after
strikers.

Born in Melbourne, Australia, on 9 October 1975, Viduka began his professional career at
Melbourne Knights, before Celtic snapped him up after witnessing his ability at Croatia
Zagreb. The move to Parkhead endured complications, which saw Viduka return home to
Australia via Zagreb, complaining of stress. Viduka eventually demonstrated his potential
during the 1999/00 season, scoring 27 goals, finishing the campaign Scotland's Player of the
Year. David O'Leary had tracked Viduka's progress for twelve months and the Leeds boss
signed his target for £6m in June 2000.

It took the Aussie time to settle at Elland Road after his debut against TSV Munich 1860, which frustrated supporters, especially when he departed after a few weeks to represent his country at the Sydney Olympics when not match-fit. However, once Viduka notched his first Leeds goal against Besiktas in the Champions League, the goals flowed.

Scoring eleven goals in seven games, including braces against Tottenham Hotspur and Charlton Athletic, Viduka became the first Leeds player since Allan Clarke in 1971 to score four goals in a match following his scintillating performance in Leeds' 4-3 win over Liverpool. The victory helped Leeds record a rare double against Liverpool, one of only three occasions in the club's history. Full of confidence, Viduka linked superbly with Alan Smith, Robbie Keane and Harry Kewell to score goals on the domestic scene and in Europe. Top scorer with 22 goals, Leeds finished fourth and stunned pundits by reaching the Champions League semi-finals.

Having impressed in Europe's premier tournament, it was no surprise when Viduka was the subject of constant transfer speculation linking him to clubs in Italy and Spain during the close season. However, committing his future to Leeds, Viduka once again finished leading scorer in 2001/02 as Leeds qualified for Europe. Unfortunately, the team's failure to make the Champions League heralded a rapid decline in the club's fortunes as finances spiralled out of control, but throughout the most difficult period in the club's history, which has seen numerous managerial changes and players depart, Viduka has led the line diligently.

In 2002/03, when Leeds flirted with relegation, Viduka's form dipped like many of his colleagues, but after the appointment of Peter Reid, Viduka responded with a blitz of goals during the run-in. Scoring 20 league goals, the first Leeds player to do so since Lee Chapman in 1990/91, fourteen came in the final ten games. In an amazing scoring spree, Viduka scored a hat-trick in a 6-1 victory at Charlton Athletic, braces against Middlesbrough, Tottenham and Fulham, and a brilliant last-minute winner at Arsenal in the penultimate game of the season, which clinched safety.

Sadly, last season Viduka was unable to save Leeds from relegation. Finishing top scorer for a fourth consecutive season is a first in Leeds United's history, but it is one record he would no doubt have traded for survival. As the club enters a new dawn Viduka has teamed up with former Leeds hit man Jimmy Floyd Hasselbaink at Middlesborough. Over the years, talented centre forwards have graced the number nine shirt for Leeds United. Mark Viduka, with 72 goals in 162 (+4 substitute) appearances, is one of them.

RUSSELL WAINSCOAT

Russell Wainscoat was one of Leeds United's most prolific strikers during the club's formative years. Indeed, prior to the Revie era, this powerful inside left was among the four most potent scorers in the club's history. Using his strength to brush aside opponents, Wainscoat was impossible to stop when bearing down on goal.

Born in East Retford on 28 July 1898, Wainscoat played for Malty Main before a dazzling Football League debut for Barnsley against Fulham in March 1920 when he scored a hat-trick. Joining Middlesbrough for £4,000 in 1923, Wainscoat moved to Leeds in March 1925 in a £2,000 transfer.

Leeds' new striker made a terrific start, scoring in his opening two games, although his debut strike came in a 4-1 defeat at Newcastle United. The second, however, heralded a 4-1 victory against Liverpool, Leeds' first win in ten games, and went a long way to ensuring his new club survived their inaugural campaign in the First Division.

The next two seasons saw Wainscoat play intermittently, but when fit he proved to be a dangerous forward. Although not prolific like Tom Jennings, Wainscoat scored consistently. In 1925/26, he grabbed five goals in consecutive games against West Ham (2), Arsenal, Manchester United and Liverpool, and the following term scored four against West Ham in the last home game of the season.

Wainscoat's endeavours made him only the second Leeds player to notch four goals in a game as Jennings had achieved the feat twice during the season. Sadly though, Leeds' 6-3 win was one of just three victories after the turn of the year and only confirmed the end of the club's first taste of top-flight football when Fairclough's charges finished in the bottom four each season.

Dick Ray was duly appointed manager for the 1927/28 campaign, which would be Wainscoat's best since arriving at the club. Striking the opening goal of the season in a 5-1 win against South Shields, two unbeaten runs bolstered Leeds' promotion drive. The first

Wainscoat heads for goal against Hull City during a league clash in 1927/28.

brought seven consecutive victories, Wainscoat scoring against Bristol City, Port Vale (twice), South Shields and Southampton. A defeat in the last home game to Manchester City cost the title but Leeds deservedly finished runners-up with Wainscoat (18 goals), Jennings, Charlie Keetley and John White scoring 78 goals.

Back in the First Division, Wainscoat struck eleven goals in Leeds' opening dozen fixtures, but with Jennings injured for much of the season, goals dried up. Finishing mid-table, Wainscoat scored 19 times, finishing second-top scorer behind Keetley. In 1929/30 Leeds surprised many sides by finishing fifth; a position not bettered for three decades. Wainscoat was top scorer with 18 goals, including braces in thumping wins against Grimsby Town 6-0 and Sunderland 5-0. He also notched a hat-trick in Leeds' 8-1 win against Crystal Palace in the FA Cup, a club record that still stands.

Unfortunately, in 1930/31, Leeds struggled despite great wins against Middlesbrough 7-0 and Manchester United 5-0, Wainscoat scoring in both games. Relegation came in the final match despite a 3-1 win against Derby County. In the shake-up that followed, Wainscoat was dropped after three games of the new campaign.

As Leeds went on to gain promotion as runners-up, Wainscoat joined Hull City in October 1931, helping his new side win the Third Division (North) title in 1932/33.

Gaining 1 cap for England against Scotland in 1929, Russell Wainscoat, who died in 1967, was a firm favourite with Leeds United supporters. Scoring 93 goals in 226 appearances, Wainscoat is tenth on the all-time list of goalscorers at the club.

ROD WALLACE

Rod Wallace was one of Howard Wilkinson's major signings during the build-up to the 1991/92 campaign. After one season back in the First Division, Wilkinson recognised that a partner for Lee Chapman was a priority, and in Wallace he had one of the best young prospects in England. The transfer fee of £1.6m set by a tribunal would be a sound investment over the coming years.

Born in London on 2 October 1969, Wallace was one of three brothers to make their mark at Southampton, creating history in October 1989 when the trio played against Sheffield Wednesday. Rod's twin brother Ray played for Leeds and Stoke City, while elder brother Danny played for Manchester United and won an England cap. Possessing dazzling pace, Rod's speed off the mark could destroy the best defenders and he could score virtuoso goals. An England Under-21 and 'B' international, Wallace struck 45 goals in 101 League appearances for the Saints.

Making an impressive debut on the opening day of the season against Nottingham Forest, Wilkinson's new strike force yielded 27 league goals as Leeds challenged Manchester United for the biggest prize in domestic football. While Chapman was the target man, Wallace was the sniper, as an athletic late volley against Everton brilliantly demonstrated. The goal came in the middle of a purple patch, which also brought goals in consecutive games against QPR, Aston Villa and Luton Town.

As the season entered the Easter fixtures, Wallace grabbed three goals in the final five games. Following a header against Chelsea in 3-0 win, Wallace's most important strike was also his most fortuitous; a crucial equaliser at Sheffield United on the day Leeds clinched the title. The most spectacular arrived in the final game when he drifted past a number of players before finishing neatly against Norwich City to complete an unforgettable season.

The 1992/93 campaign saw Wallace play in a memorable 4-3 win at Wembley in the Charity Shield, but the title defence was a disaster as Leeds failed to win away all term and only just avoided relegation. Wallace scored 7 goals, including a hat-trick at Coventry City in the final game of a tortuous season.

As Wilkinson began to rebuild his side, Wallace linked up with Chapman's long-term replacement, Brian Deane. While the new centre forward struggled to settle, Wallace had his most prolific season; top scoring with 17 league goals. Among his strikes was a superb solo effort against Tottenham Hotspur at Elland Road, which won the Goal of the Season award.

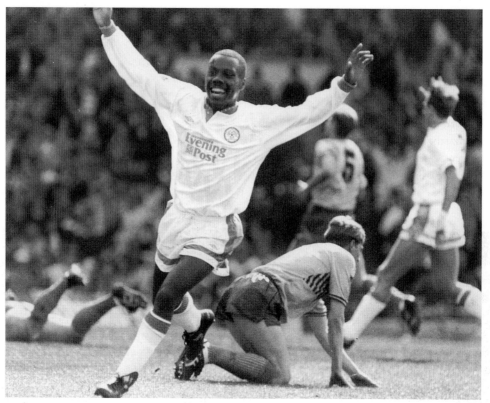

Rod Wallace after scoring the winning goal – his fourteenth of the 1991/92 season – for Leeds United against Norwich City.

Picking up the ball on the halfway line, Wallace waltzed past a number of defenders before curling the ball home.

Leeds ended the season fifth, as they did the following term, but Wallace's form and goalscoring instincts dipped markedly. Scoring just 6 goals, he missed the League Cup final at Wembley. As George Graham began the task of rebuilding the side in 1996/97, Wallace rediscovered some of his spark but it was a dubious honour to top score with 8 goals, equalling Kevin Hird's lowest tally in the club's history in 1979/80.

Finally, in 1997/98, Wallace rediscovered his best form. Linking superbly with new signing and target man Jimmy Floyd Hasselbaink, Wallace ended his final season at the club with 13 goals, scoring braces against Sheffield Wednesday and Blackburn Rovers, as Leeds qualified for Europe again. During the close season, Wallace joined Rangers on a 'Bosman', winning several honours in his three-year spell at Ibrox.

Since 2001, Wallace has played briefly for a number of clubs but it was during his days at Leeds United when he fulfilled his potential. Unfortunate not to win a full cap for England, there were few more majestic sights than Rod Wallace in full flow. Possessing superb close control and élan, 'Hot Rod', who scored 66 goals in 223 (+35 substitute) appearances for Leeds, produced many sublime moments.

DAVID WETHERALL

David Wetherall joined Leeds United as part of a combined fee of £275,000 with Sheffield Wednesday defender Jon Newsome in June 1991. With no first-team experience, Wetherall's signing was potentially a gamble, but the chemistry student made a substitute appearance against Arsenal shortly after arriving and, once his studies were complete, matured into a dependable player over a six-year period.

Born in Sheffield on 14 March 1971, Wetherall captained England Schoolboys and won a bronze medal at the World Student Games. Football, however, was always Wetherall's first-choice career and after sitting on the bench when Leeds defeated Liverpool in the Charity Shield at Wembley, he impressed at centre half towards the end of the 1992/93 campaign with a number of promising performances.

Wetherall joins the Leeds attack against Crystal Palace.

Wholehearted, a strong tackler, composed and superb in the air, Wetherall was also dangerous at set pieces and scored the first of 18 goals for the club against Chelsea. Breaking into the first team on a regular basis the following term, Wetherall was solid alongside Chris Fairclough in defence, and scored an important goal when Leeds defeated Liverpool. Finishing fifth was a great improvement on the previous campaign when Leeds failed to win an away game all season.

Early on in 1994/95, another memorable strike contributed to a fine 2-1 win against Manchester United, Leeds' first victory against their Pennine rivals at Elland Road since 1981. With Fairclough injured throughout the campaign, Wetherall was now the mainstay in the centre of defence and helped Leeds deservedly qualify for Europe.

The 1995/96 campaign from a centre-back perspective was extremely unsettled as Wetherall partnered John Pemberton, Richard Jobson, Paul Beesley and Lucas Radebe for short spells. Nevertheless, Leeds coped for much of the season, reaching a first Wembley final since 1973 and the quarter-finals of the FA Cup. Wetherall featured in every game on the road to the Twin Towers, but the League Cup final against Aston Villa ended in bitter disappointment, as did the remainder of the League campaign.

Following a dour season as George Graham took the helm from Wilkinson, Leeds came back strongly in 1997/98, qualifying for Europe once again. Among a number of rousing displays, Wetherall again thrilled Leeds supporters with a superb header to defeat Manchester United early on in the campaign. When David O'Leary succeeded Graham as manager at the beginning of 1998/99, Wetherall dropped out of the first-team picture with the emergence of Jonathan Woodgate.

After 232 (+18 substitute) appearances for Leeds, Wetherall joined Bradford City in a £1.4m deal following the Bantams' promotion to the Premier League. During an exciting relegation dogfight, Wetherall scored the crucial goal against Liverpool in the last game of the 1999/00 season, which not only saved Bradford from the drop, but also guaranteed Leeds a place in the Champions League qualifiers!

Relegated to Division One in 2000/01, Wetherall has played over 100 games for the Bantams, but his and City's immediate future is uncertain following relegation last season. David Wetherall was a fine defender for Leeds United during much of the last decade when his commitment and loyalty was never in doubt.

CHRIS WHYTE

Chris Whyte was one of the first arrivals at Leeds United following the club's Second Division title success in 1989/90. Signed for £400,000, Whyte's partnership with Chris Fairclough in central defence formed the bedrock that Howard Wilkinson could build his team on and proved a key factor in the side's ultimate Championship success.

Born in London on 2 September 1961, Whyte enjoyed something of a nomadic career after beginning his professional career at Arsenal in 1978. Despite winning 4 England Under-21 caps in 1982, Whyte found it impossible to oust future Leeds boss David O'Leary from centre-back. Prior to his arrival at Elland Road, Whyte played briefly for Crystal Palace, Los Angeles Lazers and West Bromwich Albion, where he won the Player of the Year award in 1989.

The first year back in the First Division surpassed everyone's expectations at the club as Leeds finished fourth and reached the latter stages of the League Cup. Replacing Peter Haddock at centre-back, Whyte made his debut alongside Fairclough in a 3-2 win at Everton on the opening day of the 1990/91 season and it was clear that the new central defensive pairing had potential.

A reassuring figure in defence, Whyte was a firm tackler, superb in the air, controlled a ball neatly and utilised his experience to dominate opponents with well-judged tackles and blocks. Apart from stopping opponents, Whyte was a danger at set pieces. During the campaign, his goals contributed to wins against Sunderland and Aston Villa, but the most important in the League Cup semi-finals against Manchester United counted for nothing with Leeds losing 3-1 on aggregate.

Finishing in fourth was a marvellous achievement, but nothing compared to the 1991/92 season as Leeds challenged Manchester United in the First Division title race.

Missing one match, Whyte scored once, at Notts County in a 4-2 win. The pressure was most intense during the Easter fixtures and the Fairclough-Whyte partnership was outstanding. Four matches ended in victories, with two goals conceded, and as Manchester United stumbled, Leeds won the title after a dramatic 3-2 win at Sheffield United.

Whyte played in Leeds' thrilling Charity Shield victory at Wembley at the start of the 1992/93 campaign, but with the emergence of Jon Newsome and David Wetherall, moved on at the end of the season. Playing for a number of clubs briefly, Whyte received a standing ovation from Leeds supporters when he played for Birmingham City in the League Cup semi-finals in 1996 and non-league Rushden & Diamonds in an FA Cup replay in 1999.

Affectionately dubbed 'Huggy', Whyte enjoyed the most rewarding years of his career while at Leeds. Always positive in his 146 (+1 substitute) appearances for the club, Chris Whyte's efforts during the renaissance of Leeds United in the early 1990s were superb.

HOWARD WILKINSON —————————

Howard Wilkinson masterminded the renaissance of Leeds United in less than four years after taking the helm on 10 October 1988. It was a remarkable turnaround in the club's fortunes as the team came through the wilderness years of the Second Division to land the First Division title. Organised, astute and ultra-professional, Wilkinson is the last English-born manager to win the ultimate domestic honour.

Born in Sheffield on 13 November 1943, Wilkinson made little impact during a decade as a player with Sheffield Wednesday and Brighton. However, as a coach and manager at Boston United his status developed. Wilkinson graduated in physical education at Sheffield University and taught at Abbeydale School in Sheffield. Enhancing his reputation as a coach and manager at Notts County, Wilkinson was an FA regional coach in his hometown, managed England's semi-pro and Under-21 teams prior to guiding Sheffield Wednesday to promotion in 1983/84.

Replacing Billy Bremner at Elland Road, Wilkinson guided Leeds clear of the relegation zone and prior to the transfer deadline signed Gordon Strachan, Chris Fairclough and Carl Shutt in the first stage of his rebuilding program. Finishing tenth, Wilkinson strengthened his squad further during the close season with a number of signings including Mel Sterland, John Hendrie and Vinnie Jones.

Leeds had one target in 1989/90: promotion to the First Division. As the new arrivals settled in alongside Mervyn Day, Peter Haddock, Ian Baird and David Batty, Wilkinson's reshaped team overcame a slow start to top the table by New Year. Signing Lee Chapman would be the final piece of the promotion jigsaw, despite having a substantial points lead eroded during the run-in. Leeds secured promotion and the Second Division title in the last game at Bournemouth with a Chapman header.

Adding John Lukic, Chris Whyte and Gary McAllister to his first-team pool, which also included Gary Speed and Carl Shutt, Leeds surpassed everyone's expectations by finishing fourth and reaching the semi-finals of the League Cup. The campaign was not without problems, especially at left-back, which saw Glynn Snodin, Mike Whitlow, Chris Kamara and Haddock suffer injury; in Haddock's case ending his career.

Considered dark horses for the 1991/92 Championship, Tony Dorigo solved the manager's left-back problem and Rod Wallace added extra options in attack. However, nobody predicted the head-to-head battle that would ensue between Leeds and bookies' favourites Manchester United.

With the best midfield around in Strachan, McAllister, Batty and Speed, a solid defence and hard-working attack, Leeds confounded pundits with some exceptional performances. Magnificent away wins at Aston Villa and Sheffield Wednesday stood out, but it would not be until the Easter fixtures that Leeds edged decisively ahead to clinch the title with a dramatic 3-2 win at Sheffield United in the penultimate game.

Throughout an amazing campaign, Wilkinson kept calm, outfoxing his counterpart Sir Alex Ferguson at Old Trafford with team selections and tactics. His efforts deservedly earned him the Manager of the Year award and, shortly after, Leeds defeated Liverpool 4-3 in the Charity Shield at Wembley. However, his gamble in signing the mercurial Eric Cantona disrupted the 1992/93 season as Leeds failed to win an away game all season and only just avoided relegation.

It was time to rebuild again. Wilkinson brought in numerous players, including Brian Deane, Lucas Radebe, Gary Kelly, David Wetherall and Tony Yeboah as Strachan, Chapman, Sterland, Whyte, Speed and Batty moved on. There was some success as Leeds twice finished fifth, qualifying for Europe in 1994/95, but matters came to a head in 1995/96 after the club's first Wembley final in twenty-three years.

The manner of Leeds' 3-0 defeat to Aston Villa and subsequent collapse in league form placed enormous pressure on Wilkinson. Despite signing Nigel Martyn and Lee Bowyer during the close season, the club's new owners, Caspian Group, ended his eight-year association with the club following a 4-0 defeat at home to Manchester United in September 1996. Appointed the Football Association's technical director, Wilkinson managed the England Under-21 side, and the first team as caretaker manager, but it was his years as Leeds United boss when Wilkinson was at the pinnacle of his career.

Despite some poor signings like Tomas Brolin, many more served the club with distinction. In addition, Wilkinson's youth policy produced full internationals such as Ian Harte, Harry Kewell, Alan Smith, Jonathan Woodgate, Paul Robinson and Stephen McPhail. Numerous managers succeeded Don Revie; none, however, came close to the success that Wilko enjoyed during his tenure.

Wilkinson prepares his team.

HAROLD WILLIAMS

Harold Williams came to the attention of Leeds United when he starred for Newport County in a shock FA Cup win at Elland Road in January 1949. Impressed, Major Frank Buckley signed the flying winger during the close season for £12,000.

Born in Glamorgan on 17 June 1924, Williams failed to make it at Swansea Town after trials but played as a guest for Belfast Celtic and Clintonville during the Second World War. Serving in the Royal Navy, when professional football resumed in 1946/47, Williams joined Newport, making 75 appearances during a three-year spell.

The Welshman made his Leeds debut against QPR in the opening game of the 1949/50 season and quickly settled into the side. There was a vast improvement on the previous campaign as Leeds finished fifth and reached the quarter-finals of the FA Cup for the first time in the club's history before going out to eventual winners Arsenal.

Swift, skilful, elusive and creative, Williams scored against Carlisle United, Bolton Wanderers and Cardiff City during the Cup run. In the league, he fired home 10 goals, including a brace against Coventry City in a 4-0 win. Second-top scorer behind Frank Dudley, the next two seasons would see Williams supplying crosses for Len Browning to convert as Leeds finished in the top six.

At the end of the 1952/53 campaign, Raich Carter took over from Major Buckley as manager, but it was a term to forget for Williams as he broke a leg at Everton halfway through the season. It must have been particularly frustrating watching from the sidelines as Williams had been creating opportunities for close friend John Charles following his career-changing switch to centre forward, scoring eight goals in his first half-dozen games as a striker.

Williams returned after injury on the opening day of the 1953/54 season. All sorts of records were broken as Charles scored a club-record 42 league goals. Williams assisted in many of the Gentle Giant's goals and notched 7 himself, including strikes in Leeds' 6-0 win against Notts County and 7-1 victory against Leicester City.

Finishing tenth, Leeds overcame four defeats in the opening five fixtures to miss promotion by just a point twelve months later. Carter's team made sure in 1955/56 however Williams, who played 19 games, was not in the side when Leeds pinched the runners-up spot with six consecutive wins during the run-in.

Williams had notched 35 goals in 228 appearances for Leeds but realised his days at the club were over. Returning to Newport in March 1957, Williams ended his playing days at Bradford Park Avenue in 1957/58. Winning 4 caps for Wales, this popular personality ran pubs in Leeds for many years until his retirement.

Harold Williams caused havoc for defenders with his tricky wing play as Leeds United developed from an ordinary side to one consistent enough to win promotion back to the First Division. A wonderful talent, Williams was one of the most dangerous players to represent Leeds who could be a genuine threat from both flanks.

ROY WOOD

Roy Wood was Leeds United's outstanding goalkeeper during the 1950s. A key member of Raich Carter's promotion-winning side in 1955/56, Wood rarely let the team down after he succeeded John Scott in goal.

Born in Wallesey, Merseyside, on 16 October 1930, Wood could have pursued a career in athletics or hockey, because at school he excelled in both, and while at Leeds was a renowned wicketkeeper in the Leeds and District League. However, it was as a goalkeeper where Wood made his name. Starting out as a teenager at Harrowby, Wood, who served with the RAF during the war years in the Far East, honed his skills at New Brighton and Clitheroe before signing for Leeds in May 1952.

Following his debut in a 3-1 win against Derby County in October 1953, Wood enjoyed a ten-game spell in the first team, but it would take a year for the ambitious 'keeper to stake his claim for a regular spot. It came after a 5-1 defeat at Bristol Rovers. With Leeds trying to recover from losing five of their opening six fixtures in 1954/55, the Rovers loss resulted in Wood's call-up two weeks after his twenty-fourth birthday for a clash with Plymouth Argyle, which Leeds won 3-2.

Fearless, a terrific shot-stopper and commanding in his penalty area, Wood grasped his opportunity as Leeds raced up the table and were unfortunate to miss promotion by just one point. Playing behind Jimmy Dunn, Grenville Hair, John Charles and Eric Kerfoot, Leeds were solid, letting in fewer goals in the final twenty-eight games than the previous fourteen when Wood was not between the sticks.

Expectations were high for the coming season but Leeds stuttered. Struggling for goals, Carter switched Charles to centre forward and brought the inexperienced Jack Charlton in at centre half. The tactic worked, but Leeds had a lot of ground to make up. However, in the final nine games they hit a purple patch, winning eight to snatch the runners-up spot behind Sheffield Wednesday.

An ever-present throughout the promotion campaign, Wood was now able to play against the likes of Stanley Matthews, Tom Finney, Nat Lofthouse and Duncan Edwards. Leeds got off to a fine start, winning seven of their opening ten fixtures and eventually finished in eighth place, their highest top-flight finish since 1929/30. Again, Wood was ever-present, but the loss of Charles to Juventus resulted in Leeds just avoiding relegation in 1957/58.

The following season, again Leeds struggled. Dropped after twenty-six matches following a 3-1 home defeat to Preston, a game in which Don Revie scored his first goal for the club, Wood was transfer listed during the close season. At twenty-eight, he could have carried on his career, but stunned everyone by retiring from the game. Unbelievably consistent, between

Leeds United 1956/57. From left to right, back row: Kerfoot, Ripley, Dunn, Wood, Hair, Charlton. Front row: Meek, Nightingale, Charles, Brook, Overfield.

October 1954 to January 1959, Wood missed one game at Bolton Wanderers in February 1958, playing 185 games (179 league, 6 FA Cup). In all, this popular personality made 203 appearances for Leeds.

Although not able to influence matters on the pitch, Roy Wood was not lost to the game because for many years he played a prominent role at the Professional Footballers Association. Among many aspects of the game that he improved, Wood was a member of the organisation's management committee that negotiated the abolition of the maximum wage for a footballer. One of Leeds United's most consistent goalkeepers, succeeding generations of players have benefited because of the work undertaken by one of the game's unsung heroes.

TONY YEBOAH

Tony Yeboah was a goalscoring phenomenon during his brief stay at Leeds United. Arriving in a blaze of publicity in January 1995, much was expected and Yeboah delivered. Powerfully built, the Ghanaian packed an amazing shot, which produced stunning goals. Leeds supporters recently voted his twenty-five-yard volley against Liverpool in August 1995 the club's greatest goal of all time.

Born in Kumasi, Ghana on 6 June 1966, Yeboah began his career at Kumasi Corner Stones before Saarbrucken of the German Second Division spotted him playing for Okwawa United. Honing his skills, Yeboah joined Eintracht Frankfurt, which is where this incredible striker's career took off. African Footballer of the Year runner-up in 1993, Yeboah struck 68 goals in 123 games for the Bundesliga outfit before Howard Wilkinson paid a club record £3.4m transfer fee for his services.

A daunting sight when bearing down on goal, Yeboah immediately began terrorising defences. Scoring on his debut at Old Trafford in an FA Cup defeat, Yeboah received rapturous applause against QPR when he entered the fray as a substitute. Handed a full debut against Everton, Yeboah scored the only goal of the match with a predatory strike. Leeds fans had a new hero and the chant reverberating around Elland Road was 'Yeboah, Yeboah, Yeboah'.

The win against Everton provided a platform for Leeds. Winning nine of the last thirteen games of the 1994/95 campaign, Leeds pinched a UEFA Cup spot, with Yeboah scoring 12 goals in 16 starts, including a superb hat-trick against Ipswich Town. Wilkinson's investment had proved an inspirational decision and his leading sharpshooter continued in devastating fashion at the start of 1995/96 campaign.

Scoring a brace at West Ham in a 2-1 win on the opening day of the season, Yeboah posted a candidate for the annual Goal of the Season competition in the next game at home to Liverpool with a quite spectacular strike that crashed in off the underside of the crossbar. By the end of September, there would be further contenders to consider, following an amazing thirty-yard thunderbolt at Wimbledon and an overhead special during Leeds' opening UEFA Cup clash in Monaco. Scoring hat-tricks in both games, Yeboah was the most talked about striker in Britain.

Yeboah was etching his name into club folklore. Scoring ten goals in the opening ten fixtures of the season, Yeboah joined a select group to achieve the feat at Leeds, following in the footsteps of Tom Jennings (1926/27), Gordon Hodgson (1938/39) and John Charles (1953/54).

Unfortunately, after scoring in Leeds' 3-1 victory against Manchester United on Christmas Eve, Yeboah picked up a knee injury representing Ghana in the African Nations Cup finals. Playing only a handful of league and cup matches during the remainder of the campaign,

Yeboah helped Leeds reach the quarter-finals of the FA Cup and a first Wembley final for twenty-three years after scoring in both legs of the League Cup semi-final win against Birmingham City. However, Leeds' harrowing defeat at Wembley would be Yeboah's last performance of what had promised to be a memorable season.

Top scorer with 15 goals, Yeboah won the club's Player of the Year award but his days were numbered at Leeds after George Graham replaced Wilkinson as manager. Struggling with fitness and confidence, Yeboah ripped off his shirt in frustration when substituted at Tottenham Hotspur in March 1997. It would be his last game for the club. Scoring 32 goals in 61 (+5 substitute) games, Yeboah joined Hamburg for £1m six months later. Time has not dimmed his status because Tony Yeboah was a sensational talent.

———————————————————————— # TERRY YORATH

Terry Yorath signed professional forms with Leeds United at just seventeen but like many youngsters at Elland Road had to wait some years before cementing a place in the first team. Predominately a tough-tackling midfield player, Yorath became a valuable member of the side in the mid-1970s that won a First Division Championship.

Born in Cardiff on 27 March 1950, Yorath was a promising rugby union player before he fortuitously played for Cardiff Boys when they were a player short. The outstanding footballer on the day, Yorath won 4 Welsh Schoolboys caps and after turning down offers from Bristol Rovers, Bristol City and his home-town club Cardiff City, joined the Revie revolution at Leeds.

Following his debut against Burnley in May 1968, Yorath would not get an extended run in the first team until the final games of the 1969/70 season when the League campaign was over. Spasmodic appearances would follow until 1972/73, and like so many of Revie's aces waiting in the wings, did not disappoint when called up.

During the campaign, Yorath was outstanding when he came on for Jack Charlton in Leeds' FA Cup semi-final win against Wolves, and deputised in both legs of the European Cup Winners' Cup semi-final against Hadjuk Split. Reaching two cup finals was a great achievement but they ended in heartache. Yorath featured in both, coming on for Eddie Gray in the FA Cup final against Sunderland and playing centre half against AC Milan in the European Cup Winners' Cup final in Salonika.

In many ways, Yorath had been extremely unfortunate because, having gained 8 caps, he would have walked into most First Division sides. Indeed, when Yorath made his Welsh debut against Italy in a World Cup qualifying match in November 1969, he had only played in the Leeds first team twice and made two substitute appearances!

In 1973/74, Yorath finally broke into the side following injuries initially to Eddie Gray, then Johnny Giles and to the Irishman's deputy Mick Bates. With Paul Madeley deputising for Gray, Yorath came in for Bates. In all Yorath played in five positions during the season, and impressed on the left side of midfield alongside Billy Bremner and Madeley as Leeds powered their way to a second League title.

Yorath scored twice during the League campaign, at Ipswich and the only goal against Norwich City at Elland Road. Having won his first major honour, Yorath played throughout the 1974/75 campaign when Leeds reached the European Cup final. Unfortunately, as new boss Jimmy Armfield began the process of replacing Revie's legends, Yorath became the scapegoat for a section of home supporters' frustrations, even though he always gave his best whether playing in midfield, defence or as an auxiliary striker.

Joining Coventry City for £125,000 in August 1976, after three seasons Yorath played for Tottenham Hotspur, Bradford City and Swansea City, but injuries meant he would play fewer

The United squad pose during the build-up to the 1970 FA Cup final. From left to right, back row: Reaney, Sprake, Harvey, Cooper. Middle row: Bremner, Hunter, Charlton, Madeley, Yorath. Front row: Gray, Lorimer, Giles, Bates, Clarke, Jones, Hibbit, Belfitt.

than 80 games in eight years. On the international scene, Yorath represented Wales for twelve years, winning 59 caps.

As a manager, Yorath guided a number of clubs, including Wales, whom he so nearly took to the 1998 European Championships. Currently assistant manager at Huddersfield Town, his daughter Gabby Logan is a well-known media star, but sadly, tragedy struck the Yorath family when son Daniel died of a heart condition.

Terry Yorath was a fine utility player during 165 (+32 substitute) appearances for Leeds United. Like Rod Belfitt, Terry Hibbitt and Mick Bates before him, Yorath was a testament to Revie's man-management skills and without players of his quality and loyalty Leeds would not have been the force they became.

MANAGER		CAREER	LEAGUE*	FA CUP	LEAGUE CUP	EUROPE	OTHER	TOTAL
HERBERT CHAPMAN	LEEDS CITY	1912-1919	122	5	0	0	144	271
DICK RAY	LEEDS UNITED	1920 & 1927-1935	324	18	0	0	17	359
ARTHUR FAIRCLOUGH	LEEDS UNITED	1920-1927	294	15	0	0	17	326
WILLIS EDWARDS	LEEDS UNITED	1947-1948	49	1	0	0	0	50
RAICH CARTER	LEEDS UNITED	1953-1958	210	7	0	0	0	217
DON REVIE	LEEDS UNITED	1961-1974	555	65	41	78	1	740
JIMMY ARMFIELD	LEEDS UNITED	1974-1978	158	16	12	7	0	193
ALLAN CLARKE	LEEDS UNITED	1980-1982	78	4	2	0	0	84
EDDIE GRAY	LEEDS UNITED	1982-1985 & 2003-2004	163	9	12	0	0	184
BILLY BREMNER	LEEDS UNITED	1985-1988	128	7	7	0	3	145
HOWARD WILKINSON	LEEDS UNITED	1988-1996	332	27	31	9	13	412
DAVID O'LEARY	LEEDS UNITED	1998-2002	145	11	7	40	0	203

CHAIRMAN		CAREER	LEAGUE*	FA CUP	LEAGUE CUP	EUROPE	OTHER	TOTAL
HILTON CROWTHER	LEEDS UNITED	1919-1924	168	10	0	0	32	210
HARRY REYNOLDS	LEEDS UNITED	1961-1967	231	25	15	21	0	292

OTHER: Midland League and Wartime fixtures, Charity Shield, Full Members Cup, Simod Cup, Zenith Data Systems Cup

LEAGUE: Includes five play-off fixtures in 1986/87

PLAYER	WITH CLUB		LEAGUE		F.A. CUP		LEAGUE CUP		EUROPE		CHARITY SHIELD		OTHERS		TOTAL		WAR TIME	
	FROM	TO	APPS	GLS	APPS	GLS	APPS	GLS	APPS	GLS	APPS	GLS	APPS	GLS	APPS	GLS	APPS	GLS
Neil Aspin	1982	1989	208/4	5	17	0	9	1					6	0	240/4	6		
Ian Baird	1985 & 1988	1987 & 1990	165/2	50	8	6	9	1					8	0	190/2	57		
Jim Baker	1920	1926	200	2	8	0									208	2		
Mick Bates	1964	1976	106/15	4	10/4	1	9/8	1	26/9	3					151/36	9		
David Batty	1985 & 1998	1993 & 2004	280/21	4	16	0	21	0	20/1	0	1	0	12	0	350/22	4		
Rod Belfitt	1963	1971	57/19	17	6/1	3	17/2	5	24/2	8					104/24	33		
Willie Bell	1960	1967	204	15	24	1	15	1	17	1					260	18		
Lee Bowyer	1996	2003	196/7	38	16	3	7/1	1	38	13					257/8	55		
Billy Bremner	1959	1976	586/1	90	69	6	38	3	77	16	2	0			772/1	115		
Tommy Burden	1948	1955	243	13	16	0									259	13		
Eric Cantona	1992	1992	18/10	9			1	0	5	2	1	3			25/10	14		
Lee Chapman	1990 & 1996	1993 & 1996	135/4	62	11	4	15	10	5	1	1	0	4	3	171/4	80		
John Charles	1949 & 1962	1957 & 1962	308	153	19	4									327	157		
Jack Charlton	1952	1973	629	70	52	7	35	7	56	10	1	1			773	95		
Trevor Cherry	1972	1982	393/6	24	28/1	1	35	4	20/1	2	1	1			477/8	32		
Allan Clarke	1969	1978	270/3	110	43/2	25	13	2	33	14	2	0			361/5	151		
Tom Cochrane	1928	1936	244	23	15	4									259	27		
David Cochrane	1937	1950	175	28	10	4									185	32	13	7
Bobby Collins	1962	1967	149	24	13	1	2	1	3	0					167	26		
Terry Cooper	1961	1975	240/10	7	30/1	0	21	2	48	2	1				340/11	11		
Wilf Copping	1930 & 1939	1934 & 1942	174	4	9	0									183	4	28	0
Fred Croot*	1907	1919	218	38	9	0									227	38	14	0
Tony Currie	1976	1979	102	11	9	0	13	5							124	16		
Mervyn Day	1985	1993	232	0	11	0	14	0					11	0	268	0		
Tony Dorigo	1991	1997	168/3	5	16	0	10/1	0	7	0	1	1	1	0	203/4	6		
Albert Duffield	1920	1925	203	0	8	0									211	0		
Harry Duggan	1925	1936	187	45	9	4									196	49		
Jimmy Dunn	1947	1959	422	1	21	0									443	1		
Willis Edwards	1925	1939	417	6	27	0									444	6	24	2
Chris Fairclough	1989	1995	187/6	21	14/1	0	17/2	2	5	0	1	0	8	0	232/9	23		
Brian Flynn	1977	1982	152/2	11	6/1	0	12	0	4	0					174/3	11		
Billy Furness	1928	1937	243	62	14	4									257	66		
Johnny Giles	1963	1975	380/3	88	61	15	19	1	61/1	11	2	0			523/4	115		
Arthur Graham	1977	1983	222/1	37	12	3	22	4	3	3					259/1	47		